The
Digital
Photography

The step-by-step secrets for how to
make your photos look like the pros'!

Book

VOLUME
2

Scott Kelby

The Digital Photography Book, Volume 2

The Digital Photography Book, Volume 2 Team

TECHNICAL EDITORS
Cindy Snyder
Jennifer Concepcion

EDITORIAL CONSULTANTS
David Hobby
David Ziser
Steve Dantzig

TRAFFIC DIRECTOR
Kim Gabriel

PRODUCTION MANAGER
Dave Damstra

GRAPHIC DESIGN
Jessica Maldonado

COVER DESIGNED BY
Jessica Maldonado

STUDIO SHOTS
Rafael "RC" Concepcion

PUBLISHED BY
Peachpit Press

Copyright ©2008 by Scott Kelby

FIRST EDITION: December 2007

Composed in Myriad Pro (Adobe Systems Incorporated) and Lucida Grande (Bigelow & Holmes Inc.) by Kelby Media Group.

Trademarks

All terms mentioned in this book that are known to be trademarks or service marks have been appropriately capitalized. Peachpit Press cannot attest to the accuracy of this information. Use of a term in the book should not be regarded as affecting the validity of any trademark or service mark.

Photoshop, Elements, and Lightroom are registered trademarks of Adobe Systems Incorporated.
Nikon is a registered trademark of Nikon Corporation.
Canon is a registered trademark of Canon Inc.

Warning and Disclaimer

This book is designed to provide information about digital photography. Every effort has been made to make this book as complete and as accurate as possible, but no warranty of fitness is implied.

The information is provided on an as-is basis. The author and Peachpit Press shall have neither the liability nor responsibility to any person or entity with respect to any loss or damages arising from the information contained in this book or from the use of the discs or programs that may accompany it.

THIS PRODUCT IS NOT ENDORSED OR SPONSORED BY ADOBE SYSTEMS INCORPORATED, PUBLISHER OF ADOBE PHOTOSHOP, PHOTOSHOP ELEMENTS, AND PHOTOSHOP LIGHTROOM.

ISBN 10:   0-321-52476-4
ISBN 13: 978-0-321-52476-8

12 11 10

Printed and bound in the United States of America

www.kelbytraining.com
www.peachpit.com

To Jean A. Kendra
for coming along with us
on this crazy ride, and for
being such a great friend
to our family for all these years.
We love you!

Acknowledgments

Although only one name appears on the spine of this book, it takes a team of dedicated and talented people to pull a project like this together. I'm not only delighted to be working with them, but I also get the honor and privilege of thanking them here.

To my amazing wife Kalebra: I don't know how you do it, but each year you somehow get more beautiful, more compassionate, more generous, more fun, and you get me to fall even more madly in love with you than the year before (and so far, you've done this 18 years in a row)! They don't make words to express how I feel about you, and how thankful and blessed I am to have you as my wife, but since all I have here are words—thank you for making me the luckiest man in the world.

To my wonderful, crazy, fun-filled, little buddy Jordan: You are, hands-down, the coolest little boy any dad could ever ask for, and although I know you don't read these acknowledgments, it means so much to me that I can write it, just to tell you how proud I am of you, how thrilled I am to be your dad, and what a great big brother you've become to your little sister. Your mom and I were truly blessed the day you were born.

To my beautiful baby daughter Kira: You are a little clone of your mom, and that's the best compliment I could ever give you. You already have your mom's sweet nature, her beautiful smile, and like her, you always have a song in your heart. You're already starting to realize that your mom is someone incredibly special, and take it from Dad, you're in for a really fun, exciting, hug-filled, and adventure-filled life.

To my big brother Jeff: A lot of younger brothers look up to their older brother because, well… they're older. But I look up to you because you've been much more than a brother to me. It's like you've been my "other dad" in the way you always looked out for me, gave me wise and thoughtful council, and always put me first—just like Dad put us first. Your boundless generosity, kindness, positive attitude, and humility have been an inspiration to me my entire life, and I'm just so honored to be your brother and lifelong friend.

To my in-house team at Kelby Media Group: You make coming into work an awful lot of fun for me, and each time I walk in the door, I can feel that infectious buzz of creativity you put out that makes me enjoy what we do so much. I'm still amazed to this day at how we all come together to hit our often impossible deadlines, and as always, you do it with class, poise, and a can-do attitude that is truly inspiring. You guys rock!

To my editor Cindy Snyder: I can't thank you enough for stepping up to the plate and knocking one out of the park while our "Mommy of the Year" Kim Doty was off having the cutest little baby boy in the whole wide world. You did just a great job of keeping the train on the track, keeping me focused, and making sure that volume 2 kept the same voice and vision as the original. I am very grateful to have worked on this with you. Way to go!

To Dave Damstra and his amazing crew: You guys give my books such a spot-on, clean, to-the-point look, and although I don't know how you do it, I sure am glad that you do!

To Jessica Maldonado: I can't thank you enough for all your hard work on the cover, and on the look of this and all my books. We got very lucky when you joined our team.

To my friend and Creative Director Felix Nelson: You're the glue that keeps this whole thing together, and not only could I not do this without you—I wouldn't want to. Keep doin' that Felix thing you do!

To Kim Gabriel: You're the unsung hero behind the scenes, and I'm sure I don't say this enough, but—thank you so much for everything you do to make this all come together. I know it's not easy, but you somehow make it look like it is.

To my best buddy Dave Moser: Besides being the driving force behind all our books, I just want you to know how touched and honored I was that you chose me to be the Best Man at your wedding. It meant more than you know.

To my dear friend and business partner Jean A. Kendra: Thanks for putting up with me all these years, and for your support for all my crazy ideas. It really means a lot.

To my Executive Assistant and general Wonder Woman Kathy Siler: I'm writing this right before my Bucs play your Redskins, so at this point, while we're still talking: thank you, thank you, thank you! All the mini-miracles you pull off each day enable me to continue to write books, take photos, and still have a family to come home to. I am indebted (not so much that I want the Redskins to win, but indebted nonetheless).

To my publisher Nancy Ruenzel, marketing maverick Scott Cowlin, production hound Ted Waitt, and all the incredibly dedicated team at Peachpit Press: It's a real honor to get to work with people who really just want to make great books.

To David Ziser, David Hobby, and Steve Dantzig who acted as tech editors on three very important chapters: the wedding photography chapter, the off-camera flash chapter, and the studio chapter, respectively. I asked for your help because I knew you were the best, and the book is far better because of your input, suggestions, and ideas. I am so very grateful to you all.

To all the talented and gifted photographers who've taught me so much over the years: Moose Peterson, Vincent Versace, Bill Fortney, David Ziser, Jim DiVitale, Helene Glassman, Joe McNally, Anne Cahill, George Lepp, Kevin Ames, and Eddie Tapp. I give you sincere and heartfelt thanks for sharing your passion, ideas, and techniques with me and my students. As you know—I couldn't have done it without you.

To my mentors John Graden, Jack Lee, Dave Gales, Judy Farmer, and Douglas Poole: Your wisdom and whip-cracking have helped me immeasurably throughout my life, and I will always be in your debt, and grateful for your friendship and guidance.

Most importantly, I want to thank God, and His son Jesus Christ, for leading me to the woman of my dreams, for blessing us with such amazing children, for allowing me to make a living doing something I truly love, for always being there when I need Him, for blessing me with a wonderful, fulfilling, and happy life, and such a warm, loving family to share it with.

Other Books by Scott Kelby

Scott Kelby's 7-Point System for Adobe Photoshop CS3

The Adobe Photoshop Lightroom Book for Digital Photographers

The Photoshop CS3 Book for Digital Photographers

The Photoshop Channels Book

Photoshop Down & Dirty Tricks

Photoshop Killer Tips

Photoshop Classic Effects

The iPod Book

InDesign Killer Tips

The Digital Photography Book

Mac OS X Tiger Killer Tips

Getting Started with Your Mac and Mac OS X Tiger

The Elements 5 Book for Digital Photographers

The iPhone Book

About the Author

Scott Kelby

Scott is Editor, Publisher, and co-founder of *Photoshop User* magazine, Editor-in-Chief of *Layers* magazine (the how-to magazine for everything Adobe), and is the host of the top-rated weekly video podcast *Photoshop User TV*.

He is President of the National Association of Photoshop Professionals (NAPP), the trade association for Adobe® Photoshop® users, and he's President of the software training, education, and publishing firm, Kelby Media Group, Inc.

Scott is a photographer, designer, and award-winning author of more than 40 books, including *The Photoshop CS3 Book for Digital Photographers*, *Photoshop Down & Dirty Tricks*, *The Adobe Photoshop Lightroom Book for Digital Photographers*, *The Photoshop Channels Book*, *Photoshop Classic Effects*, *The iPhone Book*, *The iPod Book*, and *The Digital Photography Book*, volume 1.

For three years straight, Scott has been honored with the distinction of being the world's #1 best-selling author of all computer and technology books, across all categories. His books have been translated into dozens of different languages, including Chinese, Russian, Spanish, Korean, Polish, Taiwanese, French, German, Italian, Japanese, Dutch, Swedish, Turkish, and Portuguese, among others, and he is a recipient of the prestigious Benjamin Franklin Award.

Scott is Training Director for the Adobe Photoshop Seminar Tour, and Conference Technical Chair for the Photoshop World Conference & Expo. He's featured in a series of Adobe Photoshop training DVDs and has been training Adobe Photoshop users since 1993.

For more information on Scott, visit his daily blog at www.scottkelby.com

Table of Contents

Chapter One   1
Using Flash Like a Pro
If You Hate the Way Photos Look with Flash, You're Not Alone

Table of Contents

Table of Contents

Table of Contents

Shooting Weddings Like a Pro
How to Get Professional Results from Your Next Shoot

Table of Contents

Table of Contents

SHUTTER SPEED: 1/60 SEC   F-STOP: F/5.6   ISO: 200   FOCAL LENGTH: 14mm   PHOTOGRAPHER: SCOTT KELBY

Chapter One

Using Flash Like a Pro

If You Hate the Way Photos Look with Flash, You're Not Alone

If you've taken a photo with your camera's pop-up flash, you're probably wondering how camera manufacturers list pop-up flash as a feature and keep a straight face. It's probably because the term "pop-up flash" is actually a marketing phrase dreamed up by a high-powered PR agency, because its original, more descriptive, and more accurate name is actually "the ugly-maker." You'd usually have to go to the Driver's License Bureau to experience this quality of photographic light, but luckily for us, it's just one simple push of a button, and BAM—harsh, unflattering, annoying, blinding light fires right into your subject's face. Seriously, does it get any better than that? Actually, it does. You just have to get your flash off your camera. Now, the first time you actually use pop-up flash and you see the quality of light it creates (and by "quality" I mean "a total lack thereof"), you'll be tempted to do just that—rip that tiny little flash right off the top of your camera (I'm not the only one who did that, right?). I have to figure that camera manufacturers include a pop-up flash on most camera models to do one thing and one thing only: spur sales of dedicated off-camera flash units (which are actually fantastic). Because as soon as you see the results from your pop-up flash, you think, "There has just got to be something better than this!" or maybe "I must be doing something wrong," or "My camera must be broken," or "This camera must have been stolen from the Driver's License Bureau." Anyway, this chapter is for people who figured there must be something better, and if someone would just show them how to use it, they could love flash again (not pop-up flash, mind you, but off-camera flash, which is a gas, gas, gas!).

1

10 Things You'll Wish You Had Known...

Okay, there aren't really 10, there are just eight, but "Eight Things" sounded kinda lame.

(1) First, go right now to www.kelbytraining.com/books/digphotogv2 and watch the short video I made to explain these points in more detail. It's short, it's quick, and it will help you read this book in half the time (that "half the time" thing is marketing hype, but you'll get a lot out of the video, so head over there first. I'll make it worth your while).

(2) Here's how this book works: Basically, it's you and me together at a shoot, and I'm giving you the same tips, the same advice, and sharing the same techniques I've learned over the years from some of the top working pros. When I'm with a friend, I skip all the technical stuff, so for example, if you turned to me and said, "Hey Scott, I want the light to look really soft and flattering. How far back should I put this softbox?" I wouldn't give you a lecture about lighting ratios or flash modifiers. In real life, I'd just turn to you and say, "Move it in as close as you can to your subject without it actually showing up in the shot. The closer you get, the softer and more wrapping the light gets." I'd tell you short and right to the point. Like that. So that's what I do.

(3) Sometimes you have to buy stuff. This is not a book to sell you stuff, but before you move forward, understand that to get pro results, sometimes you have to use some accessories that the pros use. I don't get a kickback or promo fee from any companies whose products I recommend. I'm just giving you the exact same advice I'd give a friend.

...Before Reading This Book!

(4) We don't all have budgets like the pros, so wherever possible I break my suggestions down into three categories:

 If you see this symbol, it means this is gear for people on a tight budget.

 If you see this symbol, it means photography is your passion, and you're willing to spend a bit more to have some pretty nice gear.

 If you see this symbol, it means this gear is for people who don't really have a budget, like doctors, lawyers, venture capitalists, pro ball players, U.S. senators, etc.

To make this stuff easier to find, I've put up a webpage with links to all this gear, and you can find it at www.kelbytraining.com/books/vol2gear.

(5) If you're shooting with a Sony or Olympus or a Sigma digital camera, don't let it throw you that a Nikon or Canon camera is pictured. Since most people are shooting with a Nikon or Canon, I usually show one or the other, but don't sweat it if you're not— most of the techniques in this book apply to any digital SLR camera, and many of the point-and-shoot digital cameras as well.

Here Are Those Last Three Things

(6) The intro page at the beginning of each chapter is designed to give you a quick mental break, and honestly, they have little to do with the chapter. In fact, they have little to do with anything, but writing these off-the-wall chapter intros is kind of a tradition of mine (I do this in all my books), but if you're one of those really "serious" types, you can skip them because they'll just get on your nerves.

(7) This is volume 2 of *The Digital Photography Book* **and it picks up where the last book left off** (so it's not an update of that book, it's new stuff that people who bought the first book asked me to write about next). If you didn't buy volume 1, now would be a really good time to do that (just think of it as a "prequel." Hey, it worked for George Lucas).

(8) Keep this in mind: This is a "show me how to do it" book. I'm telling you these tips just like I'd tell a shooting buddy, and that means, oftentimes, it's just which button to push, which setting to change, where to put the light, and not a whole lot of reasons why. I figure that once you start getting amazing results from your camera, you'll go out and buy one of those "tell me all about it" digital camera or lighting books. Okay, it's almost time to get to work. I do truly hope this book ignites your passion for photography by helping you get the kind of results you always hoped you'd get from your digital photography. Now pack up your gear, it's time to head out for our first shoot.

Pop-Up Flash: Use It as a Weapon

The pop-up flash built into your digital camera is designed to do one thing: give you the flattest, harshest, most unflattering light modern-day man has ever created. If you have a grudge against someone, shoot them with your camera's pop-up flash and it will even the score. Here are just some of the reasons why you want to avoid using that flash at all costs: (1) The face of the pop-up flash itself (where the light comes out) is very, very tiny and the smaller the light source, the harsher the light it produces. (2) Since the flash is positioned right above your camera's lens, you get the same quality of light and angle that a coal miner gets from the light mounted on the front of his helmet. (3) Using a pop-up flash is almost a 100% guarantee that your subject will have red eye, because the flash is mounted so close to, and directly above, the lens. (4) Because the flash hits your subject straight on, right square in the face, your subject tends to look very flat and lack dimension all around. (5) You have little control over the light, where it goes, or how it lands. It's like a lighting grenade. These are the reasons why so many people are so disappointed with how their shots look using their camera's flash, and it's exactly why using your pop-up flash should be absolutely, positively, a last resort and only done in the most desperate of situations (okay, actually it can do a somewhat decent job if you're shooting outdoors, your subject has the sun behind them, and you need a little bit of light so they're not just a silhouette. Then, maybe, but other than that…). So, what should you use instead? That's on the next page.

The Advantages of a Dedicated Flash

If you want to get pro-quality results from using flash, you're going to need to get a dedicated flash unit (like the one shown above or the ones listed below). What makes these dedicated flashes so great is:

(a) You can aim the flash in different directions (a pop-up flash just blasts straight ahead);
(b) You can angle the flash upward (this is huge—you'll see why later in this chapter);
(c) You can take this flash off your camera to create directional light;
(d) Even when mounted on your camera, because it's higher, you'll get less red eye;
(e) You get control, a more powerful flash, and most importantly, a better quality of light.

Best of all—today's dedicated flashes do almost all the work for you. Here are three I like:

Scott's Gear Finder

Nikon SB-800 (around $315)

Canon 580EX II, shown above (around $360)

Metz 54 MZ-4 [for Nikon, Canon, and others] (around $388)

Get Your Flash Off Your Camera

RAFAEL "RC" CONCEPCION

One of the best things you can do to get better results from your dedicated flash is to literally get it off the camera. That way, you can create directional light—light that comes from the side of your subject or above (or both), rather than the flat, straight-on light you get when your flash is mounted on your camera. Directional light is much more flattering, more professional looking, and it adds dimension and depth to your photos. One way to get your flash off your camera is to use a flash sync cord (a short cable that connects your flash to your camera). You just attach one end of the flash sync cord to the flash sync connector on your camera, and the other end plugs into the same place on your flash unit, and well—that's it. You can now hold your flash unit in your left hand—up high, and out away from your body. Then, aim it down at your sub-ject and you've got directional side lighting (by holding it up high and aiming it down at your subject, it kind of approximates how sunlight would hit your subject). This little change alone makes a huge difference (it's bigger than you'd think), because having that directional light is really what it's all about. Getting that dedicated flash unit "off-camera" is one of the first steps to getting pro-quality results, and all that's standing between you and having more professional-looking directional light is that sync cord (which only costs around $30 for a 5' sync cord. Worth every penny).

Making Your Flash Wireless

If you've got a recent Nikon or Canon digital SLR (anything from a Nikon D70 on up, or a Canon 20D or later), it has a feature that lets you avoid having to use a sync cable at all—you can get off-camera wirelessly instead. Once you turn this feature on, it acts just like there's a sync cable in place—when you press the shutter button on your camera, it fires the flash wirelessly. So, you save money because you don't have to buy a sync cable, you don't have to worry about your sync cable breaking or getting lost—in fact, you don't have to worry about dealing with cables at all. It's really quite brilliant. However, Nikons and Canons go about this whole wireless off-camera flash thing in a different way, so they're covered separately on the next couple of pages.

High-Powered Off-Camera Flash for Any Brand of Digital SLR

Quantum makes some serious high-end pro flash units that are very popular with pro photographers (they're higher powered flashes, almost like mini-studio strobes, are packed with pro features, and come with a number of flash accessories). I use the Quantum Qflash 5d-R, which works with most brands of digital SLR cameras, and can even be used wirelessly—you just need a wireless transmitter (attached to your camera) and a receiver (connected to the flash unit). You can find out more about the Qflash 5d-R at www.qtm.com.

Going Wireless (Nikon), Part I

If your Nikon camera has a built-in pop-up flash (you have a Nikon D70, D80, D200, or D300), you can make a Nikon SB-600 or SB-800 flash go wireless. (*Note:* If you have the Nikon D2X, D2Xs, or D3 models, they don't have pop-up flash, so you'll have to buy Nikon's SU-800 transmitter, which slides into the hot shoe on the top of your camera so you can control the power of your wireless flash.) This is a two-part setup: the first part (on this page) is what you change on the flash unit itself.

(1) On the back of the flash unit, hold the center SEL button down for a few seconds until the menu you see above appears. Use the round multi-selector to jump over to the square with the two S-shaped arrows (seen highlighted above), and press the center SEL button to select it. (*Note:* If you don't see that, you can use the plus/minus buttons on the multi-selector to toggle through the menus until it appears.)

(2) Now, move your cursor over to the far right, scroll down to Remote (as seen above right), and press the center SEL button again. Your flash is now wireless (Whoo hoo!). On the next page, we'll do the final step, which is changing a setting in the camera.

Going Wireless (Nikon), Part II

Okay, here's what we need to set up on the camera itself: (1) First, pop up your camera's built-in pop-up flash (it actually triggers the wireless flash, so if you don't have your built-in flash popped up, it won't work).

(2) Now, you need to switch your camera's pop-up flash into Commander mode, so instead of firing its flash, it only sends a small light pulse to your wireless off-camera flash unit to trigger it. To do this, press the Menu button on the back of your camera, go to the Custom Settings menu, and choose Bracketing/Flash. When the Bracketing/Flash menu appears, choose Built-in Flash, then choose Commander Mode (as shown above). Highlight the Built-in field, and use the dial on the back of your camera to toggle the setting until it reads just "--" (as shown above), which means the pop-up flash is off (except for that little light pulse, of course).

(3) Now when you fire your shutter, as long as your flash unit's sensor can see the little light pulse (it's that small red circle on the side), it will fire when you press the shutter button. You control the brightness of your wireless flash from this same menu—just scroll down to Group A and over to the last field on the right. To lower the brightness (power output), use a negative number (like –1.0, for one stop less power) or a positive number to make the flash brighter. I've put together a short video clip just to show how to set this all up at www.kelbytraining.com/books/digphotogv2.

Going Wireless (Canon), Part I

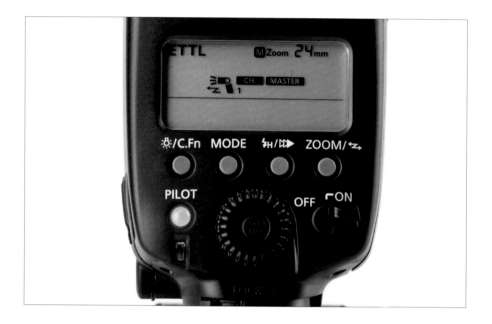

With Canon flashes, to go wireless you'll need either of the following:

(1) A Canon Speedlite Transmitter ST-E2 (around $210 at B&H Photo), which sits right on your camera's flash hot shoe, and not only triggers the wireless flash, but lets you control its brightness (power output), which is a key part of this process.

(2) You can use another Canon Speedlite flash (like a second 580EX II) as your transmitter. This second flash sits on the hot shoe on top of your camera, doing basically the same job that the Speedlite Transmitter ST-E2 does, which is to send a tiny light pulse from your camera to the wireless flash unit to tell it when to flash, and it lets you control the brightness of the wireless flash, as well.

Either way, the process is pretty similar: If you're using the ST-E2 transmitter, it's already set up as your wireless controller, and it has no flash of its own to turn off, so just put it into your camera's hot shoe and it's ready to go—you can jump over to the next page and pick up there. If you're using a Canon 580EX II Speedlite, put it in your camera's hot shoe, then hold the Zoom button on the back of the flash until the display starts flashing. Then turn the Select dial until the screen reads Master and press the center Select button. Now go to Part 2 on the next page. (*Note:* If you're using an older flash, like the 580EX, move the switch on the bottom of the flash over to Master, and you're set.)

Going Wireless (Canon), Part II

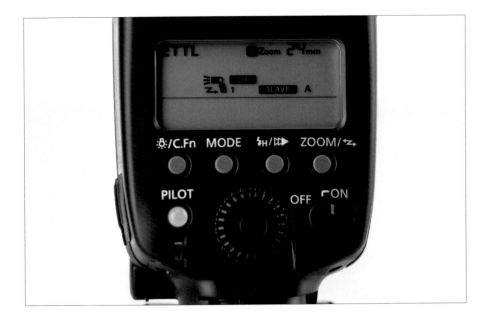

Now that you have a master flash mounted on your camera's hot shoe, you have to set up the other flash (the one you want to be wireless). (1) If you're using a Canon 580EX II Speedlite, hold the Zoom button on the back of the flash until the display starts flashing. Then turn the Select dial until the screen reads Slave and press the center Select button. (*Note:* If you're using an older Canon flash, like the 580EX, move the switch on the bottom of the flash unit itself over to Slave.) Now, to recap: The flash unit on top of your camera is set to be the master unit (the controller), and the other flash is set to be the wireless unit (the slave). (2) Turn off the flash on the master unit so it just emits a pulse of light, which triggers the wireless flash (you don't actually want it to light your subject). To do this, press the Zoom button once on the back of the flash until the display starts flashing. Then turn the Select dial until the screen reads OFF right above the word Master, and press the center Select button. I've put together a video to show you exactly how this all is done, and you can watch it at www.kelbytraining.com/books/digphotogv2.

If Your Wireless Flash Doesn't Fire

If your wireless flash isn't firing, make sure your master unit and slave unit are both on the same channel (channel 1, for example). If not, press the Zoom button twice and then use the Select dial to set them both on the same channel.

"Drag the Shutter" to See More Background

SCOTT KELBY

There are four big secrets the pros use to get beautiful quality light (and professional-looking images) from their dedicated flash units. One, you've already learned, is getting the flash off the camera so you can create directional light. The second is to set up your flash so it blends in with the available light already in the room, so the background behind your subjects looks natural. Without using this technique, you'll get what everybody else gets—the background behind your subjects turns black, they look harsh, and the shot will look pretty awful, which is why most people hate flash shots. The technique is called "dragging the shutter," and what you're doing is slowing down your camera's shutter speed so it allows in the existing light, then your flash fires to light your subject. Although this sounds complicated, it's incredibly simple. First, set your camera to shoot in program mode. Then, aim at your subject and hold the shutter button down halfway so your camera takes a meter reading of the scene. Look in your viewfinder and see the f-stop and shutter speed your camera chose to properly expose your subject, and remember those two numbers. Now, switch to manual mode and dial in those same two numbers. If the camera showed a shutter speed of 1/60 of a second, to drag the shutter you'd need to use a slower shutter speed, right? So try lowering the shutter speed to 1/15 of a second and take the shot. Don't worry—your subject won't be blurry, because when the flash fires it will freeze your subject. You'll be amazed at what just lowering the shutter speed like this will do to the quality of your flash photos.

How to Soften the Light from Your Flash

Okay, so you've used all the tricks we've covered so far, and your flash photos are already looking better—but there's still a problem. The light is still harsh because the flash itself is very small, and the smaller the light source, the harsher the light. So, to get softer, more flattering light, you need to make your light source larger, right? Right! There are a number of different tricks for doing this, and each pro does it differently, but I will tell you this—they *all* do it. They all use tricks to soften and diffuse the light from their flash (it's the third secret for getting professional-looking light from your dedicated flash). Probably the quickest and easiest way to soften the light from your flash is to snap a diffusion dome cap over the end of your flash (like the one shown above), which softens and diffuses your light. Considering how small and light it is, it does a pretty decent job. Once this cap is on, you aim your flash head upward at a 45° angle and it takes care of the rest. If you're a Nikon user and buy a Nikon SB-800 flash, it comes with the diffusion dome you see above right in the box (if you've lost your SW-10H dome, you can buy a replacement from B&H Photo). If you have a Canon flash, you can buy a diffusion dome separately, and the one I recommend is the Sto-Fen Omni-Bounce, which does a great job and is a favorite with pro wedding and event photographers (it sells for around $16.95 at B&H Photo). One thing to note: Adding this diffusion dome works great indoors, but outdoors where there's really nothing much for the light to bounce off of, it doesn't do much at all. Hey, I thought you should know.

Softer Light by Bouncing It

SCOTT KELBY

Another popular way to soften the quality of your light is to bounce your light off a ceiling. This does three wonderful things: (1) When your small, direct flash of light hits the large ceiling, it spreads out big time, so the quality of the light that falls back onto your subject is much wider and much softer. It immediately takes the harshness out of your flash, and gives you better quality light. (2) Because the light is now coming from above, it's no longer that one-dimensional, straight-on flash—now it's directional flash, which creates nice shadows and lots of dimension for your subject's face, and as a bonus (3) it keeps you from having harsh shadows on the wall behind your subject. Because the light is coming from above (down from the ceiling), the shadows appear on the floor behind your subject, not on the wall behind them. Plus, because the light is softer, the shadows are softer, too. So, if this bouncing off the ceiling technique is so great, why don't we use it all the time? Well, there are a number of reasons: (1) There's not always a ceiling you can bounce off. Sometimes you're outdoors, or (2) the ceiling is too high to bounce off of (like in a church). If the ceiling is much higher than about 10 feet, the bounce trick really doesn't work because the light has too far to travel up and back, and your subject doesn't get properly lit. Of course there's also (3) the fact that light picks up the color of what it hits, so if the ceiling is yellowish, your light becomes yellowish, and your subject will now appear (come on, say it with me) yellow-ish! However, if it's an 8'or 9' white ceiling—you're set.

Softbox–Quality Light from Your Flash

SCOTT KELBY

If you want to take this whole softening thing to the next level (qualitywise), you could buy a softbox that mounts over your flash, but the problem is they're small softboxes, so the light doesn't spread and soften as much as you'd probably like. So, what I do on location to spread and soften my light is to shoot my flash directly through a large diffusion panel, which is a large white translucent piece of fabric that spreads and diffuses the light. The one I use is a Lastolite TriGrip 33" 1 Stop Diffuser (seen above), which is very lightweight, not too expensive (it's around $67.50 at B&H Photo), and it collapses down into a very small, circular carrying case, so it's easy to take with you. To use this diffuser, have an assistant (or a friend, spouse, etc.) hold the panel about 1 foot or more in front of your flash. That way, when the tiny light from the flash hits the panel, it causes the light to spread out dramatically, which gives you much softer, smoother, more flattering light. If you don't have an assistant or a friend nearby, you can clamp your diffuser on a second light stand using a Bogen/Manfrotto mini-clamp for around $19.

Tip for Shooting Through a Diffuser

SCOTT KELBY

If you're shooting your flash through a diffuser (like the TriGrip diffuser I just mentioned), here's a tip: position the diffuser as close to your subject as possible without it actually being seen in the photo. This gives you the best quality wraparound light that is the softest and most flattering (think "closer is better"). Then position your flash so it's aimed at your subject, but still firing through the diffuser (set it at least 1 foot back from the diffuser, or even farther if you'd like softer, smoother light, but just know that the farther away you move the flash, the lower the power the light will become). From this point on, don't move the flash itself—instead just move the diffusion panel to get the light to fall where you want it to on your subject.

Where to Learn More About Off–Camera Flash

If this chapter ignites your passion for off-camera flash, and you want to take things to the next level, you'll definitely want to check out *Strobist*, which is the #1 site on the Web for flash enthusiasts (both amateurs and pros). It's run by David Hobby, a tremendous photographer and teacher who has built an entire world-wide community of flash users, and there's really nothing like it anywhere on the Web. Highly recommended (you'll find it at www.strobist.blogspot.com).

Putting That Nice Twinkle of Light in the Eyes

If you're using bounce flash and you want to add a little bit of life and sparkle into your subject's eyes, then simply pull out and raise the little white bounce card that's tucked into your flash head (well, at least it is if you're using a Nikon or Canon flash), as shown above. When you put that little white bounce card up, it redirects just enough of that light heading toward the ceiling back onto your subject to add a nice little catch light in their eyes, and the bonus is this also often removes some of the shadows that appear under their eyes. The key to making this work is that your flash head is aiming up at a 45° angle and the card is fully extended.

What to Do If You Don't Have a Bounce Card or Yours Breaks

If your bounce card is broken, or if your flash doesn't have a bounce card (hey, it's possible), then try this: use your hand. That's right—shoot with your camera in one hand, and then put your other hand up at the same position and angle a bounce card would be. It will send some of that light forward (like a bounce card), and because light picks up the color of whatever it reflects off of, your light will be nice and warm (thanks to your skin tone).

Why You Might Want a Stand for Your Flash

Most of us don't have the luxury of having an assistant to hold and position our wireless flash for us, so we either wind up holding the flash in our left hand (so our right hand is still free to press the shutter button), or we put our flash on a lightweight light stand and position it where we'd like it. You can buy a standard light stand, like the 8' Bogen/Manfrotto 306B Stacker light stand, for around $75, and then you'd need a flash shoe mount (about $8 from B&H Photo), which lets you mount your flash on a light stand like the Bogen/Manfrotto. This mount has a little plastic hot shoe on it, and your flash slides right into that hot shoe to hold your flash securely on top of the light stand. That $8 flash shoe mount is surely the inexpensive route, but the downside is you can't angle your flash head downward—only upward, and that's why the Justin Clamp, while more expensive, is really the way to go. So, once you've got your flash on this light stand, where do you put it? There's no single right answer, but I'll give you a good starting point—put it to the left, and in front, of your camera, up about a foot or so higher than your subject. That way, if you have your flash mounted on a Justin Clamp, you can aim the flash head back down at your subject, so the light is more like studio light (or window light) and helps to create that all-important directional light.

Mounting Flashes Anywhere

If you're going to wind up putting your flash on a light stand, I recommend buying a Bogen/Manfrotto Spring Clamp with Flash Shoe (better known in the industry as simply a "Justin Clamp"). This is just the handiest little gizmo and you'll love it for three reasons: (1) Your flash slides into a little plastic hot shoe on the top of the clamp, and that clamp is connected to a miniature ballhead that lets you easily and instant-ly position your flash in any direction or at any angle. So, instead of moving the light stand every time you want to change the angle of the flash, you just move that little ballhead. (2) It has a large clamp on one end, so if setting up a light stand isn't practi-cal (or isn't allowed), you can clamp it onto just about anything, from a railing, to a tree branch, to a ceiling tile. These sell for around $54 (at B&H Photo, anyway), and it's one of those accessories that once you use it, you'll never go anywhere without it.

Rear Sync Rocks (& Why You Should Use It)

SCOTT KELBY

There's a setting on your camera that will help you get better-quality photos using flash. In fact, your flash shots will get so much better that you'll wonder why this feature isn't turned on by default (but it's not—you'll have to go and turn it on yourself). It's called Rear Sync, and what it basically does is change when the flash actually fires. Usually, your flash fires the moment you press the shutter button, right? So it does freeze any action in the scene, but it also generally makes everything solid black behind your subject (like you see in most snapshots). Changing to Rear Sync makes the flash fire at the end of the exposure (rather than the beginning), which lets the camera expose for the natural background light in the room first, and then at the very last second, it fires the flash to freeze your subject. Now your background isn't black—instead, it has color, depth, and detail (as seen above right), and this gives you a much more professional look all the way around. In the example above, the shot on the left is using the normal default flash setting (notice how dark the background is, and how washed out the flash makes him look). For the shot on the right, I only changed one single thing—I switched the flash to Rear Sync. Give it a try and you'll see what I mean (just remember to keep the camera still when shooting in Rear Sync mode, because the shutter stays open longer—enough to expose for the background. This can create some cool effects if your subject is moving while your shutter is open, or it can create some irritating effects if they're moving and you don't want them to).

The Fourth Secret to Pro Flash Results

SCOTT KELBY

I saved the best trick for last (the fourth of the four pro flash tricks), and this one you can use to make your flash look like natural light. In fact, this trick works so well that if you do it right, most folks won't be able to tell that you used a flash at all—you'll just have glorious-looking, soft, natural light whenever and wherever you want it. Your goal is to create light from your flash that matches, and blends in with, the current lighting in the scene (the ambient light) and doesn't overpower it. Here's the trick: don't change your f-stop or shutter speed—instead, just lower the power output of the flash until it matches the available light. To do that, first get the flash off the camera for directional light, and diffuse the light, then take a test shot. Chances are, your flash will overpower the existing light. Now, go to your flash unit itself, lower the flash output power by one stop, and take another test shot. Look at the LCD panel on the back of your camera, and see if the light from your flash still looks obvious—like light from a flash. If it does, lower the power of your flash another ½-stop and shoot another test shot. Keep doing this (lowering the power and shooting a test shot) until you're getting just enough flash to light your subject, and nothing more. That way, it looks real, directional, and natural, instead of looking like flash (like the shot above, lit with a Nikon SB-800). It might take you five or six test shots to dial in the right amount of power, but that's the beauty of digital cameras: it doesn't cost anything to do test shots—as many as you need—until you strike that perfect balance between ambient light and the light from your flash.

Using Gels (& Why You Need Them)

The light from your flash is always the same color—white. It's nice, bright, white light, which is great in most circumstances, but what if you're doing a portrait of someone in an office, or you're shooting in a locker room, or in a meeting room? Well, that's a problem, because the color of the light from your flash won't match the color of the lighting in the room, which is exactly why some flashes (like the Nikon SB-800) actually come with pre-cut gels that slide right onto the flash to let you change the color of your flash's light, so it matches the rest of the lighting in the room. (*Note:* If you have a Canon flash, you can buy a large sheet of Rosco CTO gel for around $6.50 from B&H Photo. You'll have to cut it down in size so it fits over your flash head, but at least you'll have a huge supply of them, whereas Nikon only gives you one.) Amateurs don't worry about this, because they're going to just overpower the light in the room, right? But since you now know the pro tricks of how to balance the light from your flash with the ambient light already existing in the room, you'll need to do this next step, but believe me, for the 20 seconds it takes to slide that gel into place—it's worth it. You'd use a yellow gel for balancing your flash color with incandescent light (the standard light found in homes), and a green gel for balancing the light if you're shooting under fluorescent lights, like the ones found in most office interiors (Rosco makes those, too). Just pop that tiny gel into your diffusion dome, and you're ready to go!

Using Gels to Get That *SI* Look

SCOTT KELBY

There's a very cool trick you can do using just a yellow gel that I learned from *Sports Illustrated* photographer Dave Black when he and I were teaching a class out in San Francisco. When you try it, you'll see it has that *SI* look you see in a lot of outdoor sports portraits. It actually requires you to do two things: (1) First, you set the white balance on your camera to Tungsten (it's one of your camera's built-in white balance presets, and it makes your whole photo look very blue—well, at least it does if you're shooting outdoors), then (2) pop a yellow gel onto your flash (see the tip on the previous page to find out if you already have them or where to get them). That's it. Now, you want to shoot this near dusk, so the background sky is dark and moody. The Tungsten white balance setting makes the sky look moody and blue, but the yellow light (from the gel on your flash) hits your subject with a warm light. It's a very clever combo that is easy to achieve, and lots of pros are using this style today because, well…it's really cool (no pun intended, but I wish it had been).

If You Have to Use Pop-Up Flash, Do This

If you can't get around it, and you are in a situation where you must use your camera's pop-up flash, then at least do these two things: (1) set your flash to Rear Sync first, so you'll pick up some of the ambient light in the room, and (2) do something—anything—to soften the harshness of the flash, and that can be as simple as shooting your pop-up flash through a white table napkin or cutting a rectangle-shaped diffuser out of the side of a plastic gallon of milk and shooting through that. If you know in advance that you might have to shoot with your pop-up flash, then check out LumiQuest's Soft Screen (shown above), which is designed to fit over your pop-up flash to spread and diffuse the light. Luckily, it's very inexpensive (around $12.95), and well…if you have to use pop-up flash, this will at least make it bearable.

Two Tips for Getting Better Results from Your Pop-Up Flash

Another thing that will help you get better-looking images from your pop-up flash is to reduce the flash's brightness (lower its power) or lower your flash exposure (using flash exposure compensation). Most dSLRs have a setting where you can lower the brightness of the flash, and that helps to not blow out your subject with harsh white light. You might also try taping a small yellow gel (like a ¼-cut CTO gel from B&H Photo) over your flash and leaving it there all the time. This gives the cold flash a much warmer, more pleasing look. Thanks to flash guru David Hobby for sharing these tips.

Using a Second Flash

SCOTT KELBY

If you want to add a second wireless flash (maybe you want to use it as a hair light, or to light the background, or…whatever), it's easy. When your first flash fires, it automatically triggers the second flash so they both fire at exactly the same time. Let's say you want to add a flash to light your subject's hair. First, position the flash behind your subject, but off to the right (if you're holding your other flash in your left hand while you're shooting), as shown here. This is a perfect time to use one of those Justin Clamps I mentioned earlier, so you can clamp your second wireless flash to anything nearby, or you can position your second flash on a light stand—just make sure you don't see the stand, or the flash unit itself, when you look through your camera's viewfinder. Set your second flash to wireless mode (look back on page 9 for Nikon flashes or page 11 for Canon flashes). Best of all, you can control the brightness of this second flash wirelessly from on your camera (see the next page to find out how).

Controlling Your Second Flash (Nikon)

You will want to be able to control the brightness of each flash individually, so that way if the second flash is too bright, you can lower it without affecting the first flash or you can turn it off altogether. However, you want to be able to do all this right from your camera itself—without running around behind your subject, or running from flash unit to flash unit. On a Nikon camera, here's how it's done: On the back of the flash, set this second flash to Group B. That's all you do on the flash itself. Now, you control the brightness of each flash by pressing the Menu button on the back of your camera, going to the Custom Settings menu, and choosing Bracketing/Flash. When the Bracketing/Flash menu appears, choose Built-in Flash, then scroll down and choose Commander Mode. Your first flash (the one you hold in your left hand, or near you on a light stand) is in Group A. You set your second flash to Group B, so the brightness control for your second flash is found in the Comp field to the far right of Group B. Scroll over to that field, and to lower the brightness by one stop, dial in –1.0 (as shown above). Now shoot a test shot, and if that second flash appears too bright, try lowering it to –1.3 and shoot another test shot, etc., until it looks right. To turn if off altogether, toggle over to the Mode field, and change the setting until it reads "--" which turns off your second flash. To control the brightness of your main off-camera flash, it's controlled the same way, but in Group A. Just remember, for all of this to work, you have to have your pop-up flash up, because it triggers the flash (or you can use an SU-800 transmitter if your camera doesn't have pop-up flash).

Controlling Your Second Flash (Canon)

To add a second Canon Speedlite flash (one you'll use for a hair light or to light the background), hold the Zoom button on the back of the flash until the display starts blinking, then use the Select dial to switch the flash to Slave mode, and press the center Select button. Now your first wireless flash and this second flash will fire simultaneously, which is good, but you want to be able to control the brightness of each flash individually, right from your camera (so you're not running back behind your subject just to lower the brightness of the second flash. After all, what's the good of wireless if you have to keep running over to the flash every time you need to make a small change, eh?). To do that, you'll want to assign this second flash to a separate control group (Group B). To assign the second flash to Group B, press-and-hold the Zoom button on the back of your Speedlite, and then use the Select dial to move over to Group B. Now you can put this flash into place (behind the subject), and do a test shot. Both flashes should fire, but if the second flash (the one behind your subject) is too bright, then press the Zoom button until Ratio highlights (the ratio amount controls the brightness). Now, set the ratio to 1:2 (one stop less bright), then do a test shot. If the second flash still looks too bright (when you look at the shot in your LCD monitor), then lower the brightness to 1:4 or 1:8 and shoot another test shot, and keep this up until the second flash looks balanced. If you want to control the brightness of the first flash, make sure it's on Group A, and you can lower and raise its ratio the same way.

How Far Back Can You Stand Using Flash?

SCOTT KELBY

So, how far back can you stand from your subjects and still get pro-quality results from your flash? Well, if you're using a flash with a diffusion dome, or you're bouncing your flash, or you're using some type of diffuser to soften the light (and you should be), as a general rule, you really don't want to stand farther than about 10 feet back from your subjects. Unfortunately, any further than that and your dedicated flash won't have enough power to get the right amount of light all the way over to your subjects to light them properly.

How to Stand Back Even Farther

If you absolutely need to stand back more than 10 feet from your subject, then you can use this trick to extend the power and range of your flash: just raise your digital camera's ISO (making the camera more sensitive to light). So, if you're shooting at 100 ISO (it's always our goal to shoot at the lowest possible ISO—more on this later), then if you increase your ISO to 200, you effectively double the power (and range) of your flash. So, if you need to be 20 feet back, try increasing your camera's ISO to 200 or 400, and that should do the trick. Okay, well, there is one more thing you can try: if you don't want to raise your ISO and you have to be back farther than 10 feet from your subject, then you'll need to (gasp!) remove the diffuser cap from your flash, so your light has more power and reach (personally, I'd raise the ISO, but hey—that's just me).

How to Get More Power from Your Flash at Long Distances

If you find yourself having to shoot pretty far back (maybe you do a lot of large group shots), you might want to buy another diffusion dome cap and cut out a little section of the top so some of that light reaches a bit farther.

Controlling Your Light to Add Drama

If you want to add some serious drama and interest to your flash images, one of the quickest ways to get there is to limit the amount and shape of the light that hits your subject. By lighting only part of your subject, it puts part of your subject into the shadows, and although this is a fairly common technique using full-blown studio lighting, photojournalist David Honl has come up with his own inexpensive, lightweight light modifiers for shoe-mount flashes like the Nikon SB-800 and Canon 580EX, and I just love 'em. He's got an 8" snoot that acts like a funnel for light—concentrating it in just one area—it fits right over your flash head (as seen above) and is secured with a little ring of velcro. The snoot sells for around $23 and you can get it direct from www.HonlPhoto.com.

Shooting Sunset Portraits with Flash

SCOTT KELBY

Like a lot of shots taken with flash, this one is a formula, and if you follow it, you'll get the look you want. First, turn off your flash, switch your camera to program mode, aim at the sky (but not at the sun itself), and hold your shutter button halfway down. This tells your camera to take a meter reading of the sky, so while that button is still held down, look in your viewfinder to see the f-stop and shutter speed, and remember what they're reading (in the example above, it read f/5.6 at 1/60 of a second). Now, switch your camera to manual mode and dial in f/5.6 for your f-stop and 1/60 of a second for your shutter speed (even if you've never used manual mode before, this is a no-brainer—usually the front dial on your camera controls the f-stop, and the back dial controls the shutter speed, so just move those two dials until you see f/5.6 and 1/60 as the settings when you look through the viewfinder). Now your sunset sky will look perfect, but your subject will be almost, if not totally, a silhouette. So, turn your flash back on, but lower the brightness (power output) of the flash by around two stops, so just a little bit of flash fires—not enough to overpower the existing light, just enough to light the head and shoulders of your subject. You'll have to fire a couple of test shots to get this just right, but remember: don't change the camera settings—they're perfect as is—just lower (or raise, as the case may be) the brightness of your flash. That's it—that's how to get great-looking flash portraits at sunset. (*Note:* If the shutter speed suggested by your camera is faster than 1/250 of a second, you're hosed, as many cameras/flashes won't sync at faster than 1/250 of a second. Not all, but many.)

Chapter Two

Building a Studio from Scratch

It's Much Easier and Less Expensive Than You'd Think

It used to be that only full-time working professionals could afford to put together a studio, but these days the prices of studio gear have come down so much, and the equipment is so much easier to use, that anyone (well, anyone with a platinum American Express card) can now build a studio of their own. Of course, I'm joking, you don't have to have a platinum card (a gold card will do just fine). Actually, the main reason why building a studio from scratch is within most folks' reach today is that you can do so much with just one light. In fact, nearly this entire chapter is to show you how to get professional results using just one light. Now, in the studio we don't always refer to lights as simply "lights," because then people would know what they do (we call them "strobes," because it sounds much cooler). Studio photography is intentionally shrouded in mystery to make the process appear more complicated than it really is. In fact, there is a special committee, The Council for Creation of Complex-Sounding Studio Gear Names (the CCCSSGN, for short), whose charter is to create confusing insider lingo to throw beginners off track. For example, when we talk about the color of light, we don't use the term "indoor lighting." Nope, people would realize what that is, because they've been indoors before. Instead, we assign a color temperature measured in Kelvin, so to throw beginners off, we might say to one another, "It looks like that strobe is throwing 5500 Kelvin." And the other person might say, "It looks a bit warmer to me. More like 5900," then the other person might say, "Ya know, you might be right—it is more like 5900 Kelvin." It's amazing that either of these people ever get a date. Anyway, this chapter is designed to cut through the Kelvin and show you the light.

Studio Backgrounds

One of the least expensive, and most popular, studio backgrounds is seamless background paper. This paper comes in long rolls, and the two most popular widths are just over 4 feet wide (53") and nearly 9 feet wide (107"). The nice things about seamless paper are: (1) It's cheap. A 53-inch-wide white roll that's 12 yards long goes for around $22 (at B&H Photo), and if you want the 9-foot-wide roll, it's only around $40. (2) It's seamless. There's no visible seam where the paper folds as it reaches the floor (or a tabletop), so the background looks continuous. (3) The stands to support seamless paper backgrounds are pretty cheap, too. For example, the Savage Economy Background Stand Support System, which supports both the 53" and 107" rolls, only costs around $65. That ain't bad. And, (4) this paper comes in a wide variety of colors, from solid white to solid black, to blue, green, and everything in between (hey, that rhymes). If you're building your first studio, this is a great way to start, because you can get your background and the supports to hold it up for around $100.

So Which Should I Get, the 53" or the 107" Seamless?

If you're planning on shooting products on a table, or strictly just head-and-shoulder shots of people, you can get away with the 53" width. If you need to see more of your subjects, go with the 107".

Using Studio Flash (Called Strobes)

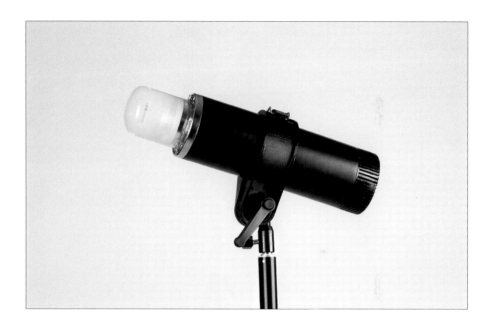

A lot of people are intimidated by studio lighting, thinking it's complicated or too technical for them, but in reality, most studio lights are just bigger versions of the off-camera
flash you're already used to (in fact, they are flashes, but in the industry they're usually
called "studio strobes" or just "strobes"). The two main differences between off-camera
flashes (like a Nikon SB-800 AF Speedlight or a Canon Speedlite 580EX II) and studio
strobes are: (1) studio strobes usually plug into the wall rather than running on batteries, and (2) studio strobes are more powerful (they put out more light) than the flash
that's on (or off) your camera. That's about it. (Well, studio strobes are usually mounted
on light stands, but since we sometimes mount off-camera flashes on light stands, too,
I think this goes in the "more in common" column.)

Scott's Gear Finder

Photogenic StudioMax III 320ws Monolight (around $260)

Elinchrom Style BX 400 Multivoltage 400ws Monolight ($549)

Elinchrom Digital Style RX 1200 1200ws Monolight ($1359)

Softening Harsh Studio Strobes

So, if the light from your regular off-camera flash is harsh, imagine how harsh the light will be from a brighter, more powerful flash (your studio strobe). Right, it's harsh city. To diffuse that light and make it softer, you have to make the light that comes from your strobe larger, because the rule is: the larger the light source, the softer the light. So, we have to put something big between our studio strobe and our subject to spread and soften that light, and for that I recommend a softbox. They're aptly named because they soften the light from your strobe big time, and they are very popular with professional studio photographers (in fact, it's the softening device of choice for most top pros). They fit right over your studio strobe (they have a hole in one end) and your flash fires through the white diffusion material at the large end of the softbox. This spreads the light, so when it hits your subject, it's a bigger source of light, and that means it's a much more flattering, softer light. But this softer light isn't just for lighting people—even if your subject is a product, you still want nice, soft shadows throughout your image, and a softbox is your key to getting just that.

Why I Prefer Softboxes to Umbrellas

©ISTOCKPHOTO/DON WILKIE

Besides softboxes, another way to spread and soften your light is to use a lighting umbrella. Surprisingly, you don't generally put the umbrella between your strobe and the subject (although you could). Instead, you turn the strobe so it's aiming 180° away from your subject—in the opposite direction. Then you put the umbrella in front of the flash (strobe) itself, so that your strobe fires into the underside of the umbrella. When the light hits the umbrella, it spreads out and travels back in the opposite direction, back toward your subject. Because the light spreads out when it hits that umbrella, the light from your strobe is much softer. So, why don't I like, or recommend, using an umbrella? It's because with a softbox your light is pretty much contained within a box—it doesn't spill out, so your light is more directional. You aim it in a direction and it pretty much goes right there. But with an umbrella, you have less control over what happens once the light leaves your umbrella. I think of it more like a lighting grenade—you throw it in the general direction of what you're trying to light, and it'll probably light it. So, while an umbrella does take the harsh light from your strobe and create soft, pretty light from it, it kind of goes everywhere. Whereas, a softbox is more contained, more directional, and you can add other accessories to narrow the throw of your softbox light even more.

What a Speed Ring Does (& Why You Need It)

So, you need: (1) a strobe, (2) a light stand to hold it up, (3) a softbox to spread and soften the light, and (4) you're also gonna need a speed ring. A speed ring is some-thing that you'd think would come standard with every softbox, because it's absolutely necessary for connecting your softbox to your strobe. These speed rings are sold separately (of course), they're generally made of a light metal, and they generally have four holes on the edge where you insert the ends of the four thin metal poles on each corner of your softbox. Once you insert those poles into the speed ring, it gives your softbox its form (it creates the shape of a box), and then you attach this whole rig (the speed ring with your softbox attached) to your strobe. By the way, when ordering your speed ring, make sure you order one designed to fit your brand of strobe. So, let's say you have a Profoto strobe, and you want to use a Chimera softbox, you'd need to either buy a Chimera speed ring that is designed to fit Profoto strobes, or you can buy a speed ring made by Profoto themselves. I would choose a Chimera model for one main reason. It's $21.45 cheaper. By the way, most speed rings are rotating (meaning you can rotate the softbox from tall to wide while it's mounted on the strobe), and if that's important to you (and I would think it would be), then make sure the one you order does rotate.

Using a Modeling Light

SCOTT KELBY

Usually, when you're shooting in a studio environment, the only lights you want to light your subject are the studio strobes themselves. Otherwise, the other lights in the room can affect your exposure, so studios are generally pretty dark once the shooting starts. This creates a problem, because the auto-focus on the camera needs some light to lock its focus onto. That's one reason why studio strobes usually come with a built-in modeling light, which is a fairly dim, continuous light that stays on between flashes to let your camera's auto-focus do its thing. Another advantage of using a modeling light is that it gives you an idea where your shadows are going to fall on your subject (it's not exact, but it does give you an idea). I leave the modeling light on all the time during a shoot, but you'll find an on/off switch on the back of your strobe unit itself (or on a separate power pack or battery pack, if you're using one).

Scott's Pro-Speak TRANSLATOR

When you're talking about studio strobes, there are basically two kinds: (1) A monolight, which is what we've been talking about here in the book, is a self-contained unit (with the power pack, flash bulb, and power controls all in one) that plugs directly into a standard wall outlet, and (2) a flash head, which is just the flash itself, and all controls are in a separate power pack or battery pack, which you plug the flash head into.

Firing Your Studio Strobe

To get your strobe to fire when you press the shutter button, you'll need to sync your camera with your flash unit, and you can do that the same way you would with your standard off-camera flash, and that's by using a sync cord. One end plugs into your camera's sync cord input, and the other end plugs into your strobe. That's it—now when you press your shutter button, your studio strobe fires. To stop the strobe from firing each time, unplug the cable.

Sometimes You Have to Buy Gear

Just so you know, I don't get a kickback, bonus, or promotional fee from any of the companies whose products I recommend. I'm just giving you the same advice I'd give a friend if we were out shooting (which is the theme behind this entire book). This is not a book to sell you stuff, but before you move forward, understand that to get pro results, sometimes you have to use (and that means buy) some of what the pros use.

Firing Your Studio Strobe Wirelessly

While sync cords are fairly inexpensive (I found the cheapest 15-foot sync cord for around $10 at B&H Photo), you're now tied to your flash unit, so there's not much freedom of movement in your studio. To get around that, you can use a wireless flash trigger, and then you can move about freely, completely untethered, unencumbered, unfettered (insert your own "un" word here), and once you shoot wirelessly like that, going back to a sync cord feels like being put on a leash. Here's how it works: to start, you need two of these wireless devices—one sits on your camera's hot shoe and transmits the wireless signal, and the other plugs into the sync input on your strobe. What I love about them is you just plug them in, turn them on, and they do their thing. There's no real configuring or messing around for this simple setup. Now when you press your shutter button, it instantly fires your strobe, even if it's across the room. As for make and model, I use the ever-popular PocketWizard PLUS II, which is a small, very lightweight, wireless triggering system that works incredibly well, is extremely reliable, very well made, and about every studio photographer I know uses a PocketWizard. They're not cheap, at around $190 each (and remember, you need two), but they totally rock.

Using Continuous Light Instead

COURTESY OF WESTCOTT

A fast-growing alternative to studio strobes is continuous lights, and with these lights there is no "flash of light"—instead, the lights just stay on continuously. This makes studio lighting incredibly easy, because what you see is what you get. I use these continuous lights in my studio (I have three of them) and on the road with my Photoshop Lightroom Live Tour, where they have nearly created a sensation, because no matter what I tell you about them here in this book, it doesn't have the impact of seeing them used live, and people just go nuts over them. The ones I use are Westcott Spiderlite TD5s (as shown above), which use daylight-balanced fluorescent light (since they're fluorescent, they produce hardly any heat—they stay nice and cool the entire time you're shooting with them, and your subjects stay cool, too). These lights are naturally softer than the studio strobes, but of course I still use them with a softbox attached, and the nice thing is the speed ring is built right into the light itself, so you don't have to buy a speed ring. Best of all—they're fairly inexpensive, and you can buy a kit, which includes a light stand, the Spiderlite TD5 fixture, a tilter bracket, and a 16x22" softbox, for around $650 at B&H Photo. Hard to beat. So, what's the downside with these lights? There's one: since there's no flash to freeze things, things need to be fairly still, because the fluorescent lights aren't as bright as the light from a strobe, so as long as your subjects don't move a whole bunch—they're awesome.

Choosing the Size for Your Softbox

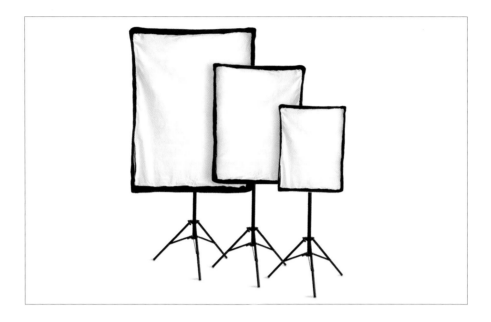

When you're trying to decide which size to choose for your softbox, there are a couple of considerations: the first being, what are you planning to shoot, and the second being, how soft do you want your light? We'll tackle the "What are you planning to shoot?" question first. If you're shooting product shots on a table, you can get away with a smaller softbox, like one that's 2x3', yet it would still be big enough to also work for head-and-shoulders portraits. If you're going to be shooting people, and doing more than just head-and-shoulder-type stuff, then you'll need to go with a larger soft-box. I mentioned before that the larger the light source, the softer the light, so if you buy a very large softbox (like one that's 3x4'), you're going to get very soft light, and you're going to be able to light a larger area. I use three sizes in my studio: a 2x3', a 3x4' for people shots, and a 7' (74") Elinchrom Octabank when I want really, really, wonderfully soft wraparound light.

Scott's Gear Finder

Photoflex 2x3' (24x32") Litedome Softbox (around $90)

Chimera Pro II 3x4' Softbox (around $180)

Elinchrom 7' (74") Octabank (around $1100)

Why You Really Need to Use a Light Meter

Shooting in the studio, with more and more lights and reflectors, can make it tricky to get the right exposure (especially when you're trying to measure light that happens in 1/250 of a second), but the pros don't sweat it because they use a light meter. They use a handheld light meter because they've already learned that their camera's built-in meter, while great for most things, just doesn't cut it in studio lighting conditions. Besides, who wouldn't want a simple-to-use device that tells you exactly how to set your exposure every time? Today's light meters are so simple to use that it's much harder not to use it than it is to use it. If you want to be a success with your studio lighting, if you want to make your life easier, and you don't want to spend all day in Photoshop trying to fix your exposure mistakes after the fact, then buy a handheld light meter. This is an absolute must (by the way, I use the Sekonic L-358 listed below).

Scott's Gear Finder

Gossen Digiflash Light Meter (around $225)

Sekonic L-358 Flash Master Light Meter (around $259)

Sekonic L-758DR DigitalMaster Flash Meter ($499)

How to Use a Light Meter

SCOTT KELBY

Before you get started, there are two simple things you do before you measure the light from your flash: (1) You enter the ISO that your camera is set to into your light meter (so if you're shooting at 200 ISO, you enter 200 ISO). And, (2) make sure the round white plastic dome on the meter is extended (turn the wheel so it extends out). That's it—you're ready to put it to use. Most people aim the light meter at the light itself, but today's meters are actually designed so they work with that white plastic dome aiming back directly at your camera's lens. If you're metering a person for a portrait, position the meter directly under their chin, with the dome aiming back directly at the camera. Now, push the button on the side of the meter, and then fire the flash (you might have to have your subject hold the meter under their chin and push the button on the side. That way, you can take a test shot to fire the flash). Once the flash fires, it instantly tells you the exact shutter speed and aperture settings you need to dial in for a perfect exposure. So you go over to your camera, make sure you're in manual mode, set your f-stop to what it said, set the shutter speed to what is listed on the meter, and you've got it—perfect exposure. As long as you don't move the light or change the power of the flash, you can continue to use those settings. If anything does change, just take a new meter reading the same way, and change your f-stop and shutter speed to match those readings.

Adding a Hair Light

If you're thinking of adding a second light to your studio, it should probably be a hair light. A hair light is just another strobe, but it's aimed directly at your subject's hair (did I even have to say that?), which helps to separate your subject from the background and give your portraits a more professional look all around. You want the light from your hair light to be pretty directional (you want it aiming right at their hair, and a little on their shoulders, and that's about it). That's why you want to buy either a very small softbox (like a 16x22" softbox—where the light, once it spreads, is just big enough to cover their head and shoulders) or a long, thin, rectangular softbox (sometimes called a strip bank) whose shallow width (no larger than 12" wide) helps to keep your hair light more directional. Also, I usually set the power on my flash unit so it's around one stop brighter than my front light, so the light from my front light doesn't overpower it.

Scott's Gear Finder

Chimera 9x36" Super Pro Plus Strip (softbox only—$175)

Smith-Victor 600-Watt Portrait Hair Light Kit w/strip bank & boom ($429)

Westcott Spiderlite TD3 Hairlight Kit w/strip bank & boom ($600)

Where to Position Your Hair Light

SCOTT KELBY

If you're going to buy a hair light, make sure you get one that either comes with a boom stand, or you'll definitely want to buy a separate boom stand for it. That's because arguably the ideal place for a hair light is to have it positioned directly over your subject's head. That way, it's easy to direct the light down exactly where you want without causing any lens flare issues from the light spilling back into your camera's lens (this is a bigger problem than you might think). When the light is aiming straight downward, it's not going to spill back into the lens, so that boom stand really makes your life easy. If you don't have a boom stand, you can still theoretically place the light straight above your subject, but you're going to see the light stand in nearly every shot, so to keep from pulling your hair out—just spring for the boom stand. Now, that being said, how far above your subject do you place the hair light? I put mine about two to three feet above the top of my subject's head, but make sure you don't position it directly over their head—it should actually be back just a little bit, so absolutely none of the hair light spills onto their face or nose.

Testing Your Hair Light's Position

SCOTT KELBY

A trick for checking the position of your hair light, to make sure none of the light from it is spilling onto your subject's face, is to turn off your main strobe (your front light), so nothing but the hair light is turned on. Your subject should be in complete silhouette, with no light on their nose, cheeks, or face whatsoever. If you see any light now, you'll need to either move your subject forward or your hair light back a little bit, until you only see light on their head and shoulders—none on the face. A trick my buddy Andy Greenwell uses is to leave all the modeling lights on, but put your hand flat out over their forehead (like you're shielding them from the light). Move your hand in toward their forehead and back out. If your hair light is in the right position, you shouldn't see any change of light on their nose while you move your hand in and out. If the light changes, then light is spilling onto their nose, so you need to move the light back just a bit.

Keeping Your Hair Light from Spilling

Probably the most popular accessory for hair lights (besides a boom stand) is an egg crate grid. This is a fabric grid that Velcros over the front of your strip bank. It narrowly focuses the light from your hair light so it doesn't spill out the sides, and it really does a wonderful job of focusing your light just where you want it. They come in different sizes, and there's one to match the exact size and shape of your strip light, but no matter what size you get—they're expensive. There must be some sort of "egg crate cartel" that controls the price of these puppies, because when you see one in person, you'd figure that it probably costs around 30 bucks, but it doesn't. An egg crate grid for a small 12x36" strip bank costs around $140, and they go up from there. Yeouch! But, once you use one, you'll always use one, because for hair lights they're absolutely ideal.

Which Mode to Shoot In

Technically, you can shoot in aperture priority (Av) mode in your studio, but if you want to make your life easier, this is the one time I would absolutely suggest that you shoot in manual mode. When it comes to using 100% flash (as we do in the studio), it's very important to be able to set both the f-stop and shutter speed independently, and manual mode lets you do just that. Your trusty light meter (the one we talked about just a few pages ago) will tell you exactly where to set those dials. Now, if you don't have a light meter (yet), and you want some settings as a starting place, try an f-stop of f/5.6 and a shutter speed of 1/60 of a second. Take a shot and see how it looks on your camera's LCD monitor. Then, don't change the settings—instead, just raise or lower the power of your main strobe until the lighting looks right to you.

A "Show Me How to Do It" Book

This is a "show me how to do it" book. I'm telling you these tips just like I'd tell a shooting buddy, and that means, oftentimes, it's just which button to push, which setting to change, where to put the light, and not a whole lot of reasons why. I figure that once you start getting amazing results from your camera, you'll go out and buy one of those "tell me all about it" digital camera or lighting books.

Where to Position Your Main Light

RAFAEL "RC" CONCEPCION

There is no absolute "right" place to position your lights (light position can be argued until late into the night), so it really comes down to how you want the shadows to look in your photo. Personally, when shooting portraits I like a "loop" lighting pattern, which is probably the most popular lighting pattern used today. To get a loop lighting pattern, you place your strobe (with a softbox attached, of course) either to your camera's left or right at about a 45° angle (or more) from you. This directional light produces a small, soft shadow on the opposite side of your subject's nose, and a triangle of light on their opposite cheek, which has a very flattering effect on most people. How high do you place this light? Ideally, you'd like it to come from above their eye level, around 3 feet higher than your lens height, so the light is casting down a little on your subject (like sunlight). How close should your softbox be to your subject? The closer it is, the softer and more wrapping your light will become, so I usually place it so close that if it were any closer it would be visible in the shot (just remember that as you move it closer, the light will be brighter. It won't get harsher—it will actually get softer, but it will get brighter). These are just the basics to get you started in the right direction—lighting is an art, and we haven't gone into broad lighting, short lighting, Rembrandt lighting, or any of the other classic styles or reasons why you place lights where you do (often depending on the shape of your subject's face), so my goal here is to give you some insights into how I light a subject, and if you came by my studio, this is the exact stuff I would show you first. Then we'd go get a beer (I mean, a Diet Coke).

Using a Fan for Windblown Effects

If you're shooting portraits of women, this is going to sound silly at first, but you want to buy a fan. Not just a fan, a powerful, hurricane-force commercial fan that would put most of your lighting equipment in jeopardy if you were to ever turn it on to its highest possible setting (which I believe, on most fans, is marked "Category Five"). Anyway, a fan with a nice kick to it (like the Air King 9212 12" Industrial Grade Electric Floor Fan, for around $65) creates a windblown hair effect that can add energy and excitement to your portraits (besides making the subject's hair look full and glamorous). The fan should be positioned on the ground, aiming upward at your subject, and once the fan is in place and turned on, there's not much else to do but shoot. If you really want to "blow people away," take a look at Buffalo Tools' 42" Industrial Fan (it sells for $325), which was designed for use in factories and sports arenas, and features high-performance, belt-driven motion with a two-speed capacitor and a thermal cut-off (whatever that means). In short, it's guaranteed to relocate anything in your studio that's not bolted to the foundation.

Want to Impress the Folks at *Vogue*? Buy This Fan!

If you get a huge, paying, fashion cover shot gig and you want to really impress your new clients, buy the only fan I've found that is made for shooting fashion—the Bowens Jet Stream Wind Machine. With its 2500-rpm blast and a wireless remote, it'll be knocking your clients off their feet (and it should—it sells for around $1,040). B&H Photo has 'em in stock. What the heck—buy two!

Want Softer, More Even Light? Feather It!

If you're already using a large softbox (one that's around 36x48" or larger), and you want softer, more even light than it delivers, then you can use a technique called feathering, which puts your subject in the softest and most even light your softbox can deliver. Feathering just means that you turn the light away from your subject, so they are now lit by just the edges of the light. They won't be getting the full intensity of the light when you feather it, so you might have to adjust your exposure so it's not too dark (use a lower number f-stop on your lens—like f/4 or f/3.5, etc.—or better yet, use your light meter and it will tell you exactly which settings to use when feathering your light). This light out at the edges of your softbox is very even, very soft, and very flattering (since the light in the center of the softbox is usually brighter and less even), so when you really need that super-soft, even light—now you know where to get it. This technique looks great on portraits of young children, a mother/daughter shot, or when you want a very soft, glamorous look to your lighting.

What That Extra Panel in Your Softbox Does

When you buy your first softbox, it may come with a second smaller diffusion panel, which you place inside the softbox (and then you place the larger outer diffusion panel on the inside edge of the softbox, to cover the front). That internal diffusion panel really serves one purpose: to try to even out the light, so you don't get a hot spot in the center of your light where the flash bulb is. This internal panel does make the light a tiny bit softer, but that's not its main job—it's to hide that hot spot. Of course, by adding this internal panel, your light has to pass through that diffusion material first, so you lose a little bit of light in the process. As a general rule, if I'm using continuous light (like the Westcott Spiderlites), I always take this extra internal diffusion panel out. That's because those daylight fluorescent bulbs are already soft (by their very nature), and the panel doesn't really soften them significantly, it just eats up light, so I especially want them out when using continuous lights, because I need all the brightness I can get. Otherwise, if I'm using strobes, I leave them in place.

Using a Pop–Up Collapsible Background

COURTESY OF WESTCOTT

Another quick and flexible studio background is a pop-up collapsible background that instantly folds up into a small, flat circle, but expands to be a full studio background in a matter of seconds. The one I use is a 5x6' Westcott Masterpiece 2-in-1 Collapsible Illuminator Background with white on one side and black on the other. It sells for around $176, and I also recommend buying the Illuminator stand to hold it up, which is another $69, but unless you can stand there and hold it up (or have somebody else hold it up), it's worth its weight in gold. So, with this background, anytime you want to shoot, you just open the round plastic case it comes in, pull it out, and it pops up, ready to go. You put it on the Illuminator background stand, and you're ready to go. Another advantage of this particular background (over the seamless paper route) is that it's very portable, lightweight, and you can set it up in literally seconds—by yourself. The only downside is it doesn't go all the way to the floor seamlessly, so it's fine for ¾-body shots, but not full-body shots. One more thing: although I use the black/white version, these collapsible backgrounds come in all sorts of patterns, looks, sizes, and colors.

The Least Expensive Extra Light

SCOTT KELBY

If you're thinking of buying an extra light, I hope it's a hair light, because if you think you need a second strobe just to fill in shadows, you really don't need one. That's because for around $30 you can pick up a silver 30" reflector, which will act as your second light by bouncing light from your first light back toward your subject to fill in any dark shadow areas. If you use the silver side of your reflector, it will throw a tremendous amount of light back at your subject (the white side reflects or bounces much less light than silver, and works best just to add a little sparkle and fill in close-up portraits). If you want a serious second-light alternative, go with a round silver reflector.

Three Backgrounds for the Price of One

One of the advantages of shooting on a white background is that you can get three different looks from it, depending on how you light it. For example, if you put two bright strobes (or continuous lights, for that matter) aiming at the background behind your subject (or product), the background will look bright white. If you dim those lights, or remove one, then the background looks like a light gray. If you leave the background lights off altogether, your white background will now look medium gray. So, with white you get three separate looks: bright white, light gray, and dark gray—all based on whether, and how, you light the background.

Using Off-Camera Flash to Light Backgrounds

If you want to add a light to your background (aiming back at your seamless paper), but you don't want to go through the extra expense of adding a second studio strobe, if you have a standard off-camera flash (like a Nikon SB-800 or a Canon 580EX), you're in luck. You can set either of these off-camera flashes to become wireless slave flashes, meaning that when your studio strobe fires to light your subject, it automatically triggers your off-camera flash to light your background. You only have to do two things to make this happen: (1) Put your flash on a light stand. (*Note:* If you have a Nikon SB-800 flash, it actually comes with wonderful little flash stand that lets you set your flash on the floor. Then you aim the head back up at your background, and this will work in a pinch.) So, the first thing (once again) is to put your flash on a light stand, and position it directly behind your subject so your subject's body hides the flash from view. Then, (2) set your off-camera flash to Slave, so it fires when it senses the light from your studio strobe. For example, on a Nikon SB-800, you'd press-and-hold the center Select button on the back of the flash unit, and it brings up a new set of menus. Make your way to the Wireless icon (the one with two S-shaped arrows), and choose that. Then move your cursor over to the right side, and scroll down to Slave. Choose Slave, and you're ready to go.

The Advantage of Shooting Tethered

SCOTT KELBY

If I'm shooting in a studio, I'm shooting tethered. This means I've attached a USB cable to my camera, which means the shots I take don't go onto my camera's memory card—instead they go from my camera straight onto my laptop computer. That way, I can see each image appear at a very large size right on my computer screen while I'm shooting. At this large size, you can really see what's going on in your photo (and how your lighting looks), and you can make adjustments based on a larger-sized 8x10" image, which makes it hard to look at that tiny 2½" or 3" LCD display anymore. When you're shooting tethered like this, you see everything (including lots of things you might have missed). I highly recommend giving tethered shooting a try. You just plug one end of your USB camera cable into the USB slot on your computer. Then the other end plugs into the USB slot on your camera. However, to shoot tethered, you'll need some software. If you're a Canon shooter, you've already got it—it's that EOS Viewer software you got when you bought your camera (if you can't find it, don't worry—you can download it free from Canon's website). If you're a Nikon shooter, then you need a piece of software called Nikon Camera Control Pro, which lets you capture your images straight to the computer, bypassing your camera's memory card altogether. It's $69.95, but you can download a working 30-day trial from Nikon's website. *Warning:* Once you shoot tethered, and can see everything so clearly and detailed, you're going to have a hard time going back to viewing your images on that tiny LCD screen. Hey, such is life, eh?

Getting Super-Saturated Background Color

SCOTT KELBY

If you want some really vivid, punchy colors as your background, here's a recipe to get just that: Start on a background of black seamless paper (I know, it sounds weird that we start creating vivid colors with a black background, but believe it or not, this is the easiest way), and then position a light on the background. Now, for a background light you can use another of the same strobes you already have (so, basically, you're going to need a second strobe if you want to light the background, or there's a trick you can pull to use your off-camera flash as a background light that we talked about a couple pages ago). Once you've got your black seamless paper in place and a second strobe (or off-camera flash) positioned behind your subject, aiming at the background, the trick is to put a vivid-colored gel (a translucent piece of plastic) over the front of your flash, and when your background flash fires, the color it produces is rich, vivid, and sur-prisingly colorful. You can get these gels (made by Lee or Rosco) from B&H Photo for around $6.50 for a 20x24" sheet (choose really vivid colors—reds, yellows, greens, etc.).

Lighting a White Background

When you shoot on a white seamless-paper background, you'll probably be surprised to find out that most of the time it doesn't look white—it looks light gray. To get it to look solid white (that nice bright white you're used to seeing in portraits and product shots), you have to light the background. It doesn't take a bunch of lights—usually just one or two will do the trick, and they don't have to be very high-powered strobes either (see the off-camera trick a few pages back), so it's not a bad idea to buy a lower-powered, less expensive strobe just for lighting the background. But beyond just having a background light aimed at your white seamless background, there's a little trick you'll want to use to make sure that the light does make the background look that nice solid white, but without blowing out the background so much that the back light starts to wash out the edges of your subject (this happens more than you might think). The pros' trick to getting around this is (you guessed it) to use their light meter. They hold the meter up against the background, aim the white dome back towards the camera position, and check the reading. You want the background to be around one stop brighter than the light on your subject. So if your meter showed f/11 for your subject, you want the background to read one stop brighter (like f/16). You get that background brighter by increasing the power (brightness) of the strobe itself. Try increasing a bit, then recheck the background with your meter again, and keep adjusting the power of the background light until it reads that one stop (or slightly more) than your subject. That's the formula.

Which Color Reflector to Use

Outdoor   Studio   Both

Reflectors come in a variety of colors (white, black, silver, gold, etc.), and if you're wondering which color does what, well, here ya go:

- **Silver** reflects the most amount of light, and doesn't change the color of the studio light that hits it, so you see a lot of portrait pros using silver.
- **White** reflectors don't bounce nearly as much light, but they're still used in portraits, and work both indoors and outdoors. White reflectors are also a good choice if you're doing product photography.
- **Gold** reflectors are for outdoor portraits to match the warm color of sunlight. They don't work well in a studio, because when the white light from your strobe hits the gold reflector, it becomes very yellow (so one side of your subject's face looks studio white, and the shadow side looks overly yellow).
- A **Black** reflector actually absorbs light, so it's used to cut reflections when you're shooting anything that's reflective, like glass, or jewelry, or tableware, or anything that's clear, etc.

For my studio portraits, I use a reflector that is silver on one side and white on the other, and I use the silver side around 80% of the time.

Where to Position a Reflector

Reflectors are a key part of a studio setup, because they keep you from having to use a second light. Luckily, they're pretty inexpensive (the Westcott 30" Silver/White Illuminator square reflector I use costs only around $43), but once you've got one, where do you put it? There is no one "right" place to position your reflector, but since its job is to bounce some of the light from your studio strobe back into the shadow areas of your subject, you'll need to position it where it can do its job, right? The first thing to remember is that the reflector normally should be placed a little forward of your subject, so the light can bounce back onto them. One popular method is to place the reflector directly beside your subject (and just a little bit forward) on the opposite side of your strobe (softbox), so it catches the light and fills in the shadows. So, if your light is positioned to the left of your subject, then the reflector would be positioned on the right side of the subject, aiming directly at them (as shown above). Another popular place to position a reflector is below your subject, aiming back at them, so the light bounces back to light their face, in particular the eyes and the shadows under the eyes. You can have your subject hold the reflector, you can position it on a stand, or even lay it on the floor in front of them. The key thing to remember with reflectors is: if the light isn't hitting the reflector fairly directly, it's got nothing to bounce, so make sure that wherever you position it, the light from your strobe is hitting it directly.

Reflectors Without an Assistant

If you don't have an assistant to hold your reflector in the studio, then it pays to buy a light stand with a reflector boom arm, so you can position (and tilt) your reflector just the way you want it. The one I use is made by Impact, and you can buy it in a kit that comes with a 32" 5-in-1 reflector (silver, white, gold, soft gold, and translucent) for around $95 at B&H Photo. The boom arm has two clips on it that hold your reflector, and because it's on a boom, you can easily tilt it to an angle you'd like. This is incredibly handy to have around (and much less expensive than hiring an assistant to hold your reflector).

Visit B&H Photo's New York Superstore

If you're ever in New York City, make it a point to drop by the B&H Photo store. It is absolutely amazing. It's like Disneyland for photographers. I could spend a day there (and I have). Anyway, they're good people.

Seeing the Light from Your Reflector

SCOTT KELBY

So, you're standing there holding a reflector. How do you know if it's really hitting your subject? Here's a quick trick for helping you position the angle of your reflector so you know the light is hitting where you want it to. Hold the reflector by its side and tilt it up and down a few times as you're facing your subject, and you'll see the reflected light move across their face. By tilting the reflector up and down a few times, you'll locate that "sweet spot"—where the light is hitting and fully bouncing from—and then you can tilt the reflector to right where you want it.

Where to Go to Learn More About Studio Lighting

If this chapter gets you excited about what can be done with just one strobe (or one strobe and a hair light), and you want to learn more (and learn how and when to add more lights), then check out the book *Softbox Lighting Techniques for Professional Photographers* from Stephen Dantzig (published by Amherst Media).

Keep Light from Hitting the Background

SCOTT KELBY

If you want to create a portrait with dramatic lighting, the key is to control where the light goes, so only a small portion of it actually hits your subject (and little or none winds up lighting the background). The problem is that even with a softbox (which is fairly directional compared to an umbrella), the light aiming back at your subject can spread too much, so we use "black flags" to block the light from hitting our background (or anything else we don't want it to hit). These flags are really just tall, or wide, black rectangular reflectors that absorb and block light, so you put one between your strobe (softbox) and the background, and voilá—it stops the light from spilling (as shown above). So, if you have more than one, you can really keep your light pretty much directed just where you want it, by putting these black flags up to block any extra light. I use two Westcott 24x36" black flags and they come in a kit called Fast Flags, which comes with two metal frames, four different flags (including two black flags), and a carrying case, for around $214. If you're not ready to plunk down that kind of change, you could always get two large black pieces of poster board or foam core, and that will do the trick.

Chapter Three

Shooting Portraits Like a Pro

More Tips to Make People Look Their Very Best

Getting professional-looking shots of people is harder than you might think, for one simple reason: the pros hire really good-looking models, and as you know, models are models for one simple reason—they forget to eat. I'm joking, of course. They're models because they photograph really, really well. So, what makes our job so hard is that we're not surrounded by fabulous-looking models who just happen to be standing around not eating. Nope, we usually wind up shooting portraits of our friends, many of whom (on a looks scale) fall somewhere between Mr. Bean and Jabba the Hut. This is why our job, as portrait photographers, is actually substantially more challenging than that of a seasoned professional—we've got to make magic from some seriously un-model-like people. This is precisely why we're often so disappointed with our portraits (when it's really not our fault). So, in this chapter we'll look at two proven strategies to get better, more professional-looking portraits every time, including: (1) how to make friends with better-looking people (it helps if you're rich), and (2) learning to control your light and pose your subjects so that no one gets a really good look at them. The key to this is to use dramatic light, and by "dramatic light" I mean—virtually none at all. The less you light these "un-model-like" subjects, the better your final images will be. In fact, think silhouette or long distance night photography, where your subjects are 100 to 200 yards away—anybody looks good from that distance (that's why long distance relationships work so well). Anyway, what this chapter will give you is a strategy for photographing people, and a list of places where good-looking people hang out and wear jeans that cost more than the gross national product of Luxembourg.

71

Don't Leave Too Much Headroom

SCOTT KELBY

When your average person takes a snapshot of someone, they almost always leave way too much space above their subject's head (as you see on the left here). It's a classic mistake most amateurs make, but luckily it's one that's really easy to fix. Just don't do that—don't leave too much space. If you remember my portrait composition tip from volume 1 of this book (position your subject's eyes at the top one-third of the frame), then you'll usually avoid this "too much headroom" problem altogether.

Shoot in Portrait Orientation

DAVE MOSER

Most photos are taken in horizontal (landscape) orientation, and that makes perfect sense, since cameras are designed that way—to be held horizontally—and that's why the shutter button is on the top right, right where your finger would naturally be. However, professional portraits are generally taken using a vertical orientation (that's why it's referred to as "portrait orientation," but that term is most often seen when you go to print something on your computer—you'll see a button for Land-scape [wide] or Portrait [tall]). So, if you want more professional-looking portraits, turn your camera vertically and shoot in portrait orientation (of course, like any rule, there are exceptions, some of which you'll learn later in this chapter).

Shooting Portraits? Get a Battery Grip!

SCOTT KELBY

If you shoot a lot of portraits, you're going to be spending a lot of time with your camera flipped vertically, and before long you'll get tired of reaching over the top of your camera to press the shutter button. When that happens, you'll want to get a vertical battery grip. Besides enabling you to use two batteries, so you can shoot longer without recharging your batteries, there's another huge advantage to battery grips, and that is that most include a vertical orientation shutter button and dials for setting your aperture and shutter speed, so you're as comfortable shooting vertically as when you're shooting horizontally. Besides those advantages, most of the photographers I know swear that it makes the whole camera feel better and more substantial in their hands, even when shooting horizontally (and how a camera feels in your hands is very important). The best news is these battery grips are available for most dSLRs, and for all the advantages they offer, they cost less than you'd think (starting at around $100). Just one thing to look for when ordering yours: not all battery grips have the vertical shutter button, so check to make sure the one you order does.

Most High-End Cameras Already Come with a Vertical Shutter Button

If you've got a high-end digital camera, like a Canon 1D Mark II or Mark III, or a Nikon D2Xs or Nikon D3, they already come with a vertical shutter button built right in. Hey, ya pay that type of money, they oughta come with one, right?

The "Sun Over Your Shoulder" Rule Is Bogus

©ISTOCKPHOTO/IZABELA HABUR

You may have heard of the "Sun Over Your Shoulder" rule, which basically states that when you're shooting people outdoors, you put the sun behind you (over your shoulder), so your subjects' faces are lit. This is a perfectly fine rule for people taking snapshots, but it is the worst thing you can do for your group portrait (besides the "tall people in the back" thing). If you want more professional-looking shots of people outdoors, the last thing you want is the bright sun blasting them straight in their faces (although that's exactly what your average person does), so everyone is squinting, trying to shield their eyes, and turning away from the camera. Worse, it puts harsh, direct, unflattering light on them. Instead, position your subjects with the sun behind them (not behind you), so it puts a nice rim light effect around them (outlining their hair), and then use just a tiny bit of flash (keep the brightness of your flash low) to put just enough light into their faces to make them blend in with the natural light that surrounds them.

Shoot Wide and Push in Tight

SCOTT KELBY

This is a concept—shooting on-location portraits with a wide-angle lens—that I hadn't considered for many years because of the time-honored rule that states: "Don't shoot people with a wide-angle lens because they look all distorted and weird." But it was one of the world's top shooters, the brilliant Joe McNally, who totally busted that myth and totally changed the way I shoot environmental portraits by turning me on to "shoot wide and push in tight." When you're shooting wide-angle and you get really close to your subjects (you're pushing in tight), they don't look distorted—only the stuff at the very edges of the frame looks a little "wide," but it's that stuff at the edge of the frame that shows the environment where the shot is taken. I was skeptical until Joe challenged me to pick up a *People* magazine and look at what most of the shots are—taken in tight with a wide-angle lens. I was shocked, but it's not just *People*, it's just about everywhere—from magazines to billboards to prints ads to the Web. The pros are shooting wide and pushing in tight. You can, too!

Name–Dropping Disclaimer

Throughout this book, I wind up mentioning names of some famous photographers. The reason I do this isn't to drop names; instead, it's to give credit where credit is due. If I learned a tip or technique and I can remember who taught it to me, I think it's only right to give them the proper credit.

Shoot Profile Shots in Horizontal

SCOTT KELBY

So, now that we've learned the Shoot Portraits Vertically rule, let's break it! (That's the great thing about the photographic rules—once you learn 'em, you can break 'em, then it's cool. It's only uncool when you break the rules by accident because you didn't know any better.) Anyway, one place where we intentionally break this rule is when we're shooting a profile view of our subject. The reason is this: because your subject is facing the edge of the frame, if you shoot your subject vertically, they look boxed-in, and that's uncomfortable for your viewer. So, by breaking the vertical rule and shooting profiles horizontally, it gives your subject some visual breathing room and makes your subject look more comfortable within the frame.

Shoot Long for More Flattering Portraits

SCOTT KELBY

Have you ever seen a high-end photo shoot on TV (maybe a fashion or celebrity shoot), and have you noticed how far back the photographer is from their subject? That's because they're taking advantage of "lens compression" offered by a longer zoom lens (which is very flattering to portraits). The shots above really tell the story—the one on the left was shot with a 50mm lens, and the one on the right with a 70–200mm lens zoomed out to 190mm. Even though all the camera settings and lighting are identical (they were taken just seconds apart), her features in the shot on the right look much more pleasing. That's why you'll see many pro photographers shooting portraits at the far range of their zoom. By that I mean they shoot with the lens extended out as far as it can go. So, if they're shooting a 28–135mm lens, they're shooting out in the 100mm to 135mm range to get the best, most flattering look for portraits.

Scott's Pro-Speak TRANSLATOR

The phrase we use for shooting all the way out at the longest end of a telephoto lens (for example, shooting at 200mm on a 70–200mm lens) is "racked out." So, you might hear a photographer say, "I shot racked out to 200," which means he shot with his lens extended out as far as it can go—to the far end of its range (in this case, 200mm).

Why Diffusers Rock for Outdoor Portraits

SCOTT KELBY

When it comes to really harsh, unflattering light for portraits, it's a toss-up between which is worse: your camera's built-in pop-up flash or direct sunlight. Luckily, as you learned in volume 1, if you're shooting portraits outdoors and there's an area with some shade nearby, you can shoot there. But what if you're out at the beach, or in the desert, or one of a thousand other places that doesn't have a shady tree nearby? Then you'll want to own one of these—a 33" Lastolite TriGrip 1 Stop Diffuser (the same one I mentioned in the flash chapter for diffusing harsh light from an off-camera flash—so it does double-duty here). Just have a friend hold this diffuser between the sun and your subject (as shown above), and instantly you have soft, beautiful, natural light on location. It sells for around $68 at B&H Photo, and you'll want this lightweight lifesaver with you every time you leave the studio.

Making a Better Background for Portraits

The key to great backgrounds for portraits is "less is more." If you're shooting an environmental portrait (a photo taken on location in someone's home, office, etc.), to get
that pro look, it's not what you do to the background—it's what you take away from
the background that makes it work. You want to have as few distracting elements in
the background as you can, so either position your subject on a very simple, uncluttered background to begin with, or if that's not possible, remove as many distracting
elements (or knicknacks) as your subject will let you get away with as I did in the
image on the right here. Don't take this lightly—to create a really great environmental
portrait, it can't just be the foreground that works. The whole photo has to work together, and by choosing (or creating) a sparse, uncluttered background, your chances
of having a winner go way up.

Trendy Composition Tip

SCOTT KELBY

Since most photos you see are either horizontal or vertical, doing something different looks…well…different! And right now, a very popular technique for portrait photography is to turn the camera at an angle, which puts your subject kind of up in the corner. The technique couldn't be simpler—just rotate your camera to the left or right a little bit and then take the shot. It may take you a couple of tries to get your subject positioned right where you want them in the frame, but this look (which has been around for years) is getting very popular once again.

Cropping Off the Top of Their Head

SCOTT KELBY

This is the next step past "Don't leave too much room above your subject's head" in portraits. In this composition technique, you actually cut off the top of your subject's head, and while that probably sounds weird reading it here, it's a very popular pro technique that fills your frame with your subject's head. Getting in tight like this makes for a very compelling look, as you see above, and now that it's been brought to your attention, you'll see this composition technique is everywhere and has become the mainstay of many top fashion, beauty, and portrait shooters. (*Note:* Although it's perfectly fine to cut off the top of their head, or side of their arms, shoulders, hair, etc., you shouldn't cut off their chin. People are actually very used to seeing the top cut off and it looks natural, but seeing a shot where the chin is cropped off makes for a very uncomfortable composition.)

Group Photos Are Easier Outdoors

©ISTOCKPHOTO/ALDO MURILLO

Lighting a group shot, and getting a consistent amount of light on each person, can be pretty challenging, which is why, when it comes to group shots, you'll usually get better results by moving the group outside. It's easier to light the group using available outdoor light, especially if you can get them in the shade (not deep in the shade, just on the edge of the shade, but without letting any dapples of light appear on them through tree branches or gaps between windows or buildings). If you're lucky enough to wind up shooting a group portrait on an overcast day, then your job will be pretty easy—just get them outside and the overcast sky will take care of your lighting woes, so you can focus on getting them posed. (By the way, professional-looking group shots never start with the photographer saying, "Okay, all the tall people in the back row.")

Tip for Posing Group Portraits

SCOTT KELBY

The next time you're shooting a group portrait, rather than lining everybody up in rows (which you already know doesn't look good), instead try to get them to rally around something—some object—and they'll arrange themselves naturally around it. For example, try posing people in and around a couch, a column, a chair, a car, a desk, or any object that can pull them together into a group that isn't just a bunch of people standing in straight lines.

Great Tip for Casual Group Shots

SCOTT KELBY

Want to make a more compelling look for a casual group shot? Put your subjects in a very tight pyramid shape (a triangle), but by tight I mean so tight that they're all touching—arms around one another, their heads very close together, with one person at the top of your frame, and one on either side of the bottom of the pyramid shape (as shown above), with the others all scrunched in the middle. Also, you'll notice their bodies are not in a straight line—they're kind of staggered, but they're all leaning into the shot, which gives the shot more energy and a sense of fun. I wouldn't try this for an executive group portrait, but if you've got a fun-loving casual group, this is a great way to visually say that about them.

Don't Use Rows—Use Clusters

If you're shooting a large group, instead of posing everyone in those tired rows, group people together in small clusters—like a mini-triangle within the group, with three or four people in each triangle. These little mini-clusters add closeness and energy, and then when you've got two or three groups put together, slide them all a little closer together to visually make one big group. (These mini-clusters don't have to touch each other—small gaps between them are okay.)

Don't Light Your Entire Subject Evenly

SCOTT KELBY

When people look at a photo, their eye is first drawn to the brightest thing in the photo, so you only want the brightest light falling where you want them to look, right? Right. So, if you're shooting a portrait, do you want the person viewing the portrait to look at your subject's face or their folded arms? Right. But most people light the entire portrait with the same exact light throughout, where the subject's hands at their sides have the same approximate light as the subject's face. If you want to create portraits that really lead the viewer to where you want them to focus, light your subject so the light is brightest on their face, and it gradually falls off the lower down their body it goes. This adds interest, drama, and a visual focus that you'll find so often in high-end portraits. By the way, this is another case for feathering your light, so that the edges of the light are what light your subject's face, and below that the light falls off pretty rapidly (but don't let it get too dark—it should still have light, and detail, just not as much as their face).

Don't Let Too Much Light Fall on Their Ears

If there's a part of your subject that doesn't need to be well-lit, it's their ears. Ears are often distracting because they're poking out of what is usually a darker area (a person's hair), so they catch enough light to draw your attention. Since a person's ears are rarely their best feature, you don't want your viewer's eyes stopping on them first, so just be careful to not have some really bright ears in your portraits.

Want Better Portraits? Don't Count Down!

SCOTT KELBY

If you want that really posed look, then count 1-2-3 right before you press the shutter button. It's almost a guarantee that you won't have any natural expressions in your portraits. It's your job as photographer to find that moment when your subject looks natural, and capture that moment in time. Anyone can stand there and say "1-2-3" and push the shutter button at "4," and if you do that, you'll wind up with images that anyone can take. If you want something special, something more natural—a genuine smile or expression—then ditch the 1-2-3 cliché and instead just talk to your subject. Engage them, get them talking, laughing, smiling naturally in the course of a conversation, or even goofing around, and then when the moment is right—capture that moment. Then you'll be giving them more than a well-lit, totally posed photo. You'll give them something special.

Shoot Before the Shoot and Between Shoots for More Natural–Looking Portraits

A number of pros swear by this technique for getting more natural shots: they tell the subject not to pose yet, because they're just taking "test shots" to check the lighting. Since you're not really shooting, they're not really posing, and you're just talking to them, firing away the whole time. Once you tell the subject, "Okay, here we go," they change their demeanor, and begin "posing," so make sure you get lots of these candid, non-posed shots before the official shoot and between shoots, because they will probably be the most natural, un-posed shots of the day.

Window Light: Where to Position the Subject

DAVE MOSER

Window light, especially light from a north-facing window, is among the most beautiful light for portraits anywhere (in fact, some pros insist on only using natural window light for all their portraits—period!). The window diffuses the light streaming in, and the larger the window, the more soft and diffuse the light. So, if you've got some nice window light, where do you position your subject to make the most of this beautiful light? You want to position your subject with their shoulder facing the window (so the light comes across your subject, creating soft shadows on the far side of their face). Then, place them about 6 feet from the window, so the light is very soft and wraps around your subject (if you get them any closer, that soft light could turn very contrasty fast). Also, position your subject a little bit back behind the window, so they catch the edge of the window light and not the direct sunlight. This edge light is very soft and gives you that wonderful, almost magical light that so many pros swear by.

Window Light: Where You Should Shoot From

DAVE MOSER

When shooting a window-light portrait, you want to set up your camera right near the window, with your shoulder facing the window. Then, you'll aim back a little toward your subject, who should be positioned just past the window, about 6 feet from it (so basically, you're up against the window, shooting at a slight angle back toward your subject).

Six Quick Tips for Fixing Facial Challenges

©ISTOCKPHOTO/EDUARDO JOSE

You can hide or greatly reduce many typical facial problems (like a big nose, round face, wrinkles, big ears, etc.) by how you pose and light your subject. Here are seven quick posing tips to help you make your subjects look their very best: (1) If your subject is balding, shoot from a lower angle, and don't use any hair light whatsoever. (2) If your subject has lots of wrinkles, try lighting them straight on, because side lighting tends to accentuate the shadows and make the wrinkles more prominent. (3) If your subject has large ears, pose them so they're only showing one ear, then light them so that ear appears on the shadow side of their face (so basically, only one ear is showing, and that one is kind of hidden in the shadow). (4) If they have a big honkin' nose (that's a technical term, by the way), then have them turn their head straight toward the camera, have them raise their chin a bit, and shoot from a little lower angle, which will take much of the emphasis off their schnozz. (5) If your subject has a double chin, have them look straight at the camera, and extend their head forward toward the camera a bit. This stretches and tightens the skin under their chin. Also, if you light them straight on (with the light positioned directly above where you're shooting from), this puts a shadow under their chin and helps to hide the double chin. (6) If your subject has a round or fat face, make fun of them, and tell them to lose a few pounds. Then, when they burst into tears, you'll have some of the most natural-looking expressions of the day. Or, you can have them turn their face to the left or right, giving a $^3/_4$-view of their face, which will make their face look less round, but really—it's your call.

Don't Shoot with Their Shoulders Straight On

SCOTT KELBY

Everybody—women, men, kids—looks better when posed with their shoulders angled toward the camera. If their shoulders are straight toward the camera, it makes your subjects look very wide and flat, and even somewhat confrontational. But by simply having them turn one shoulder away from the camera, it makes them look thinner and generally gives them a more pleasing look by lessening the width of their shoulders, and focusing more attention on their head. Remember: Their head can still face the camera—you're just turning their shoulders.

Making Your Subject Look Slimmer

SCOTT KELBY

If you want to make someone's body look slimmer, keep their arms from touching their body—leave a little gap between their arms and their body, so their arms don't add to their body mass and make their whole figure look larger. You'll see this trick used often in celebrity and fashion shots, and you'll be surprised what a difference this little gap between the arms and waist can make (as seen in the before/after above). Another trick is to have your subject face their body away from the camera at an angle, and then just twist the upper half of their body toward the camera (leaving their lower half still facing away). Again, this is one of those little tricks that makes a big difference.

Using a Posing Chair

SCOTT KELBY

One of the best reasons to pose your subjects in a chair is that people often feel more comfortable in a chair, and if they're comfortable, your chances of getting a relaxed, natural portrait go way up. If you have your subject standing alone in the middle of a studio, with all sorts of lights aimed at them, you're giving your subject every oppor-tunity to be uncomfortable, and that usually translates to less-than-natural, uncom-fortable-looking portraits. By the way, if you do shoot your subject seated, here's a tip to help get better-looking poses: have them sit near the end of the chair (being that far from the back of the chair almost ensures that they won't slouch or lean back), and it helps the overall look to have them lean a little forward, into the camera. So, the next time your subject looks really uncomfortable, offer them a seat, and watch them instantly become more comfortable, which usually results in better, more natural-looking portraits.

Keeping Your Subject "In the Zone"

DAVE MOSER

When you're shooting a person's portrait, it's a very vulnerable, and often uncomfortable, position to be in, and in most cases the person you're shooting wants you, the photographer, to be happy with what you see and what's going on with the shoot. If they feel things aren't going well, they start to think it's their fault. You want them feeling great—you want them confident and happy, enjoying their time in front of the lens as much as possible, because that translates into better portraits. One way to keep them "in the zone" and engaged is to keep talking to them. All the time. The entire time. Talk about what you're doing, why you're doing it, talk about the weather—anything to keep them engaged. Anytime there's a period of silence, they start to get worried something's wrong, and that it may be their fault. They have no idea what you're seeing through the viewfinder, and if things get quiet, they start to get concerned and they start to get edgy, and within a minute or two they're totally out of the zone. When I'm shooting a portrait, I'm talking to them the whole time. If I stop to move a light, I tell them why (I know they don't care, but I'm keeping them engaged in the shoot). I keep giving them constant verbal encouragement ("That looks great. Fantastic! Right on the money! What a great smile," etc.) the whole time, and it makes them more comfortable and confident.

Avoid Dappled Light

SCOTT KELBY

If you read volume 1 of this book, then you already know about putting your subjects in the shade to get better portraits outdoors (ideally, out near the edge of the shady area for the best light), but when you do this, there's something to watch out for—the dreaded "dappled light." That's those small areas of bright sunlight that break through the trees, causing uneven hot spots of light on your subject, which pretty much ruin the portrait (even if the dapples don't fall directly on their face). Luckily, the fix is amazingly easy—just reposition your subject in an area of the shade that doesn't have any of this distracting dappled light shining through. You can see how much better this looks in the image on the right here. Now, there are certain instances where dappled light works when you're shooting landscape photography, but when it comes to shooting people, dapples pretty much ruin any hope of a professional look, so be on the lookout for them anytime you're shooting under trees, or in a barn (where sunbeams can come through the cracks in the wood), or anyplace where small beams of sunlight can fall directly on your subject.

Window Light: Where to Position the Reflector

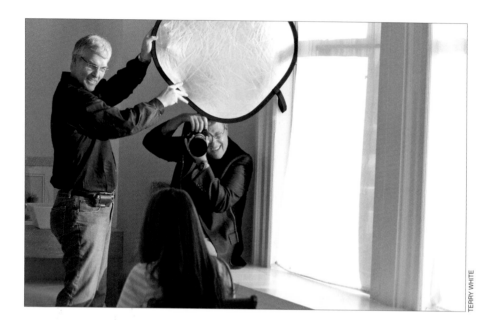

Since we generally use a reflector to bounce light into the shadow side of our subject's face, you might think that with window light you'd put the reflector on the shadow side of your subject's face. It makes sense, right? Right. And you can do that, but with window-light portraits, try this technique I learned from legendary portrait and wedding photographer Monte Zucker: bounce the light from the camera position (near the window) above your head, bouncing the window light down onto the dark side of your subject's face to open up those shadow areas.

Get Couples Really, Really Close

SCOTT KELBY

When you pose a couple and tell them to get in nice and close to each other (which you definitely should), they never get nearly close enough to look "close" in a photo. When you put your eye up to the viewfinder, you'll see the gap I'm talking about, so you tell them to "get even closer" and they move in all of about 2 inches, but I've got a trick that fixes this every time. Go ahead and take a quick shot—with the gap between them—then take it right over and show them the gap on your LCD monitor. Once they see it (and how big the gap that they thought wasn't there actually looks), they'll really get in close, and it literally makes the shot. I've done this again and again, and it always works like a charm.

Which Color Reflector to Use

One of the most popular color combinations for reflectors is silver on one side and gold on the other. The silver side is usually used when shooting indoors or inside a studio. The gold side is usually used outdoors, and since it's gold (and light picks up the color of whatever it hits), the light it throws will be very warm—like sunlight. So why wouldn't you use this warm reflected light in the studio? Because the light in your studio is usually very white balanced, probably from a flash, and you don't generally want to have white-balanced light from a flash on one side of their face and warm, golden light on the other side.

Shoot Outdoor Portraits Shallow

SCOTT KELBY

If you're shooting a portrait outdoors, for a more professional look, you want to direct the attention to your subject, minimize distracting backgrounds, and you want to put some visual separation between your subject and the background. The easiest way to do all of this is by creating a shallow depth of field. To do that, switch your digital camera to aperture priority mode, and then set your camera's f-stop to either the lowest or next-to-lowest f-stop you can. (So, if the lowest number you can go is f/2.8, you'd use f/2.8 or the next highest number, f/3.5.) Using these low numbers throws the background out of focus, which puts all the focus on your subject. This out-of-focus background look is a very popular technique used by portrait professionals when shooting outdoor portraits.

Minimizing Shadows Under the Eyes

SCOTT KELBY

If your subject starts to get shadows under their eyes (from overhead lighting in-doors or outdoors), one way to reduce those is to put a silver or white reflector directly in front of them at their chest (or as high up as right under their chin), aiming up at them and reflecting some of the light back up into their eyes.

SHUTTER SPEED: 1/160 SEC   F-STOP: F/8   ISO: 100   FOCAL LENGTH: 16mm   PHOTOGRAPHER: SCOTT KELBY

Chapter Four

Shooting Landscapes Like a Pro

More Tips for Creating Stunning Scenic Images

In volume 1 of this book, I had a chapter on shooting landscapes, and it turned out to be one of the most popular chapters in the book. So, when I started on volume 2, I knew right then I would have to include another chapter with even more landscape techniques. And the only way to come up with new landscape techniques is to (you guessed it) shoot more landscapes, and what better place to shoot landscapes than at a landscape photography workshop? So, since I published the last edition of this book, I've taught at photography workshops in beautiful locations like Yosemite National Park, Cape Cod, Great Smoky Mountains National Park, and Glacier National Park, and then I just did some shooting in Maine this summer, and some other amazing places like Utah's Monument Valley, and the Grand Canyon, and a half-dozen other incredibly scenic spots. But when it's all said and done, do you know what all these places really meant to me? Tax deductions. That's right, because I went to these locations on business (the images will be used by me to teach photography), I get some really juicy write-offs for these trips. For example, you see that photo on the facing page? That's The Wave, which is just outside Page, Arizona, and not only is access to The Wave tightly restricted by the Bureau of Land Management, it was a grueling two-hour hike in scorching 112° desert heat over rocky mountains and hot desert sand, lugging all my camera gear, tripod (and bottles of water), and I have to be honest with you—there were times when I almost gave up, but you know what kept me going? It was the fact that if I didn't get there, and get a decent enough shot to make it into this book, I couldn't write my trip off as a tax deduction. See, I really do care.

The Secret to Shooting Sunsets

Because you're shooting into the sun, it can really throw your camera's built-in light meter way off, and what looked so beautiful when you were standing there comes out…well…pretty lame. Luckily, there's a simple trick to getting perfect sunset shots every time. The trick is to aim just above the setting sun itself (but make sure you can't see the sun itself through your viewfinder), then hold your shutter button halfway down, which tells the camera to set the exposure for just what it sees in the viewfinder right now. This gives you a perfect sunset exposure, but don't let go of that shutter button quite yet (keep it held down), then you can move your camera and recompose the shot as you'd like it to look. By keeping that button held down, you've locked in that perfect exposure, and once everything looks good to you, just press the shutter button down the rest of the way and take the shot. You will have nailed the exposure and captured the scene perfectly.

Cutting Reflections in Water

SCOTT KELBY

If you're shooting streams or lakes, or really anything with water, there's a filter you're going to want to use that does something very important—it removes the reflection of the sky from the water and lets you see through the water. That way, things like rocks below the shore or in a stream, fish in a koi pond, etc., all suddenly appear crystal clear, and that can make for some very compelling images. The thing that surprises most folks is that it's a filter that most photographers use to get bluer skies—a circular polarizer. As I mentioned in volume 1 of this book, a polarizer is indispensable for getting those blue skies, but it's just as important for this overlooked double-duty of cutting reflections. Here's how it works: screw the filter onto your lens, aim at the water in front of you, and then rotate the circular ring at the end of the filter, and as you do, you'll almost magically cut through the reflections and see right through the water, as seen on the right here. It's one of those things you really just have to try to appreciate it, but believe me—you'll love it.

For Landscapes, You Need a Clear Subject

SCOTT KELBY

One of the things that kills a lot of landscape shots is that there's no clear subject, and for a landscape shot to really work, you have to be able to look at it and explain what you shot in one simple sentence. It's a lighthouse. It's that seagull on the rocks. It's that old barn. It's the palm trees on the beach. If you can't explain your landscape shot in a short sentence like that, you don't know what the subject is, and if you don't know, people viewing your image won't know either, and if that happens, the photo just isn't working. Keep this in mind when you're composing your landscape shots, and ask yourself the question, "What's my subject?" If you can't come up with a solid answer immediately, it's time to recompose your shot and find a clear subject. It makes all the difference in the world.

Using Your LCD Monitor Outdoors

RAFAEL "RC" CONCEPCION

If it's bright outside, you're going to quickly run into one of the biggest challenges of shooting outdoors, and that is you can't see anything on your LCD monitor—the sunlight washes everything out. In fact, it's often so hard to see anything that you might as well turn off your monitor and save your battery, but then your LCD monitor becomes about useless. That's why I've fallen in love with the Hoodman HoodLoupe Professional. You wear this around your neck (when you're shooting outdoors), then you simply hold it up over your LCD monitor and its soft rubber enclosure blocks out the sun and gives you a crystal clear view of your monitor. I carry this with me to all my outdoor shoots, and after you use it even once, you won't want to be without it. (*Note:* Even though it's called a "loupe," it doesn't really magnify your image like a traditional loupe—it just blocks the sun out, but really, that's all we need.) It sells for around $65 at B&H Photo.

How to Shoot a Panorama That Works

OVERLAP   OVERLAP   OVERLAP

SCOTT KELBY

In volume 1 of this book, I gave you the seven or so things you needed to do to shoot a wide panoramic image that would actually stitch together seamlessly inside Adobe Photoshop CS or CS2. It absolutely required you to shoot on a tripod (no exceptions), and switch your camera to manual mode, and your focus to manual, and a few other critical setting changes, and if you followed each and every one to the letter, Photoshop would do a pretty decent job of stitching your panorama together. But, that all changed with the introduction of Photoshop CS3. Its built-in panorama-stitching feature is so incredibly brilliant that you can literally throw out every rule from volume 1, except one. Now you can handhold your shots (no problem), use program mode or aperture priority (or whatever mode you like), you can leave your white balance set to Auto (or whatever you like), and you can pretty much just point-and-shoot, as long as you do just one thing: overlap each shot by around 20%. So, for example, if you're shooting a wide panorama, you'd start from left to right, taking one shot—let's say there's a tree on the far right side of your frame when you take that shot—then, when you move your camera over to take the next shot, that same tree should now be in the far left of your frame (so you're overlapping by at least 20%, as shown above). That's the key—overlapping—so I take a shot, move to the right, take another, and another (I've shot as few as three photos to make a pano and as many as 22), and Photoshop will put them together into one nice, wide pano for me (simply because I overlapped by around 20%).

How to Have Photoshop CS3 Put It Together

As long as you overlapped each frame of your panorama by 20% or more, Photoshop CS3 will not only stitch the photo together seamlessly, it will blend the color of the photos so they're consistent through the whole pano. Once you've taken your overlapping shots, open those images in Photoshop CS3. Then go under the File menu, under Automate, and choose Photomerge. When the dialog above appears, click on the Add Open Files button, leave the Layout (on the left side of the dialog) set to Auto, then click OK. That's it. Sit back and relax because Photoshop CS3 will do the rest, and before you know it, you'll see a stunning, wide, perfectly stitched panoramic image. This alone is worth upgrading to Photoshop CS3 for. It's that good! (*Note:* If you're thinking, "I have Photoshop CS2. That should work, right?" The answer is: Only if you follow the seven steps I outlined in volume 1 of this book. Without following those to the letter, your chances of getting a nicely stitched pano, without obvious seams and color shifts, are very slim.)

Shoot Fast When Shooting Landscape Panos

If there are any clouds in your scene when you're shooting your pano, then you'll want to shoot fairly quickly (with only a second or two between shots), because the clouds may be moving, and if you let them move too much (by taking too long between shots), they won't line up exactly, and then you'll have to spend a bunch of time retouching and cloning them to make it look right. Basically, if you're shooting a seven-photo pano, it should take you only around 10 to 12 seconds to shoot it. It should go like this: shoot, move to the right, shoot, move to the right, shoot, etc. As soon as your camera gets in place for the next frame—shoot. It sounds hard on paper, but it's simple to do in person, and because it takes so little time, you'll wind up shooting more panos, which is a good thing.

A Timesaving Pano Trick

SCOTT KELBY

When you come back in from your shoot, if your shoot included some panos, you're going to quickly find out one of the hidden challenges of shooting panos: finding them. For example, when you open your images in Adobe Photoshop Lightroom, or Adobe Bridge, or in iPhoto, etc., you're looking at thumbnails of perhaps hundreds of images from your shoot, and it's a bit of a challenge to figure out where your panos start and end. In fact, numerous times I've been looking through thumbnails from a shoot, and I look at a shot and think, "What I was thinking when I took this one?" Only to find out later it was one frame from a 10-frame pano. Worse yet, if I'm shooting on vacation, it might be a week or more before I get home to look at the images, and I completely forget that there's even a pano included in a particular shoot, because they just don't jump out at you. Luckily, there's a simple trick that makes finding your panos a two-second job: Before you shoot the first frame of your pano, hold your finger up in front of your lens and take a shot (as you see in the first frame above). Now start shooting your pano. Once you finish shooting the last shot of your pano, hold two fingers in front of the camera and take another shot (as seen in the last frame). Now, when you're looking at your photos in a photo browser and you see one finger in your shot, you know there's a pano starting there. So, select all the photos that appear between your one-finger shot and your two-finger shot—that's your pano. Open those in Photoshop CS3 and let it stitch them together for you.

The Trick for Using a Fisheye Lens

SCOTT KELBY

Fisheye lenses are making a big comeback, and they actually can be very cool for a variety of landscape shots—you just don't want your final image to look rounded and distorted, like many fisheye shots you see. You only want a very wide field of view. The trick to doing that is to simply keep the horizon line in the center of your image. This limits the amount of fisheye-like distortion and makes a huge difference in the final look. The best way to test this is to actually tip your camera downward, then back up towards the sky, all while looking through the viewfinder. You'll see the edges of your image distort as you move up and down (as seen in the top image), but you'll notice that as your horizon line gets centered in the image, the fisheye distortion is at its very minimum (like in the bottom image), and it just looks like a really, really wide-angle lens. Give it a try—you'll see what I mean (by the way, this is the only time you really want the horizon line in the center of your image, as you learned in volume 1).

When to Shoot Streams

SCOTT KELBY

If it's a gray, cloudy, rainy day (I don't mean pouring rain—a light drizzle or soft rain), then head to a local stream, because you're about to make some magic. The overcast, cloudy, rainy sky does two things that make it ideal for shooting streams: (1) it makes the rocks, leaves, and everything sticking out of the stream nice and wet, which looks great in stream photographs, and (2) it makes the scene much darker (and the darker it is while still daylight, the better), which lets you use long shutter speeds, and it's those longer shutter speeds that give the stream that wonderful silky-water effect. Try shooting in aperture priority mode, and set your aperture (f-stop) to f/22 (or a higher number if your lens has it). With this darker sky, f/22 will leave your shutter open long enough to give you that silky-water look. The shot above was taken on a drizzly afternoon where there was literally nothing else to shoot, and shooting at f/22 in the forest, under that dark, cloudy sky, left my shutter open for 13 seconds (in aperture priority mode, you pick the f-stop and then your camera will leave the shutter open for however long it takes to get the right exposure—in this case, I stood there in the gentle rain for 13 seconds. How do you like the way that phrase "gentle rain" made the experience sound? Actually, I was cold and wet, but cold, annoying rain just doesn't paint a pretty picture—but the camera sure captured one).

Don't Stop Shooting at Sunset

SCOTT KELBY

More and more people have totally embraced the golden rule of landscape photography, which is to only shoot when that wonderful, magical light is available, and that only happens just before and during dawn, and just before and during sunset. However, a lot of folks pack up their gear just a few minutes after the sun has gone down, and the sad part is, they're about to miss what is often the most magical light of all. Around 20 to 30 minutes after sunset, sometimes the clouds turn bright orange, or deep red, or purple, or if you're lucky, a combination of all three, and some of my all-time best shots have been taken after everyone else has gone to dinner. Wait even longer (30 to 45 minutes or more after sunset), and the sky will often turn a vibrant, deep blue (not black, like the night—I'm talking blue—and it happens right before night). It only lasts for a few minutes (10 or 12 minutes usually), but what wonderful twilight photos you can get then. Try this blue twilight-hour shooting when you have a cityscape, or bridge, or other lit object in the background—it makes for a wonderful scene.

Remember, Your Camera Has Similar Settings

If I'm talking about white balance, and I'm showing the Canon white balance menu, but you're not shooting with a Canon, simply breathe deeply and say to yourself, "It's okay, my [insert your camera name here] also has a white balance setting and it works pretty much like this one." Remember, it's about choosing the right white balance, not exactly which buttons to push on your camera.

How to Shoot Fog

SCOTT KELBY

I love the look of fog or mist in images. To me, it adds mystery and intrigue to the scene, but one unfortunate side effect is that it also is very hard for your camera's built-in light meter to read properly, so you get what you're seeing with your naked eye. Of course, like so many things, there's a trick of the trade that helps you get a good exposure that keeps that foggy look. Start by aiming at the fog itself, and then hold your shutter button halfway down (which tells your camera to take a reading of that area). Now, go to your camera's exposure compensation control and increase the amount of exposure by one stop (basically, what you're doing is disagreeing with what the camera read for the fog, and overriding it by increasing the exposure by one stop). On Nikon cameras, you do this by holding down the exposure compensation button on the top right of the camera (just behind the shutter button), and while you're hold-ing that button down, turn the command dial on the top back of the camera to the right until you see +1 in your camera's viewfinder. On Canon cameras, you'll hold the same button (it's in the same place—behind the shutter button), and then you'll spin the quick control dial (the big one on the back of the camera) to the right until you see +1 in the camera's viewfinder. Just one reminder: when you're done shooting your fog shots, set your exposure compensation back to zero, or you'll be shooting the rest of the day with every shot overexposed by one stop.

Getting Shots of Lightning (Manually)

©ISTOCKPHOTO/MORITZ VON HACHT

Shots of lightning can be very dramatic, because usually we only see lightning for a fraction of a second. If you can freeze that moment, it makes for a fascinating photo, but like many landscape shots, it requires a certain amount of timing (and luck). Now, before I share how to capture lightning with your camera, I want to make sure you don't capture lightning with your body. Don't stand in the rain, or under a tree, etc. Shoot from a very safe distance (because lightning will see you as a portable lightning rod) and exercise the same caution you would if you weren't a distracted photographer. Now, on to the technique. First, put your camera on a tripod (this is a must). Then, set your mode to bulb (the B setting on some cameras), which leaves the camera's shutter open for as long as you hold down the shutter button. Now, you can't actually press the button on your camera—for this to work properly you need to use either a shutter release cable (a cable that attaches to your camera with a shutter button you hold in your hand) or a wireless shutter release (you can find these for most camera makes and models at B&H Photo). The reason is: any minor vibration while your shutter is open, and the shot will be so blurry, it will be unusable. So, set up on a tripod, compose your shot (aim your camera in an area where you've been seeing lightning), use f/8 as a starting place, make sure your camera is set to bulb mode, then when you see a strike of lightning, press-and-hold the shutter release cable (or wireless) shutter button down and when you see a second strike, wait just a moment and then release the shutter button. It may take you a few tries at first, but you'll get it (hopefully the shot, not the lightning itself).

Getting Shots of Lightning (Automatically)

©ISTOCKPHOTO/ALLEN JOHNSON

If you try some lightning shots and fall in love with this type of photography, you might want to consider buying a Lightning Trigger (they're not cheap—so make sure you're truly "in love" first). This unit sits on your camera and it has a sensor that detects the bright flash of light from lightning, so it opens the shutter at exactly the right moment and gets the shot for you. In fact, you can pretty much set up your camera, set your camera to shutter priority mode (with your shutter speed anywhere from $\frac{1}{8}$ to $\frac{1}{4}$ of a second), aim in the right direction, sit back with a cool drink, and wait for the magic to happen, knowing that your camera is doing all the hard work for you. Later, when you're showing off your amazing work, there is no obligation (from the manufacturer's point of view) for you to tell the people viewing your work that you used a Lightning Trigger. Hey, it's just another tool in your bag of tricks. Go to www.lightningtrigger.com for a model that works with most cameras (it runs around $329 direct from the manufacturer. Hey, I told you it wasn't cheap).

A Trick for Shooting Great Rainbows

SCOTT KELBY

Want to really bring out the vibrance and color of your shots that have a rainbow in them? Then use a circular polarizer (now we've got three reasons to have a polarizer: [1] bluer skies, [2] cutting the reflections in water, and [3] making your rainbows "pop!"). Just turn the circular end of the filter while you're aimed at the rainbow and stop when the colors look their most vibrant. Easy enough to do, and the results are worth it. Now, beyond that, there's a wonderful tip I learned from my buddy, and renowned landscape photographer, Bill Fortney. Bill says, "If you see a rainbow, drive like the devil until you find something interesting for the rainbow to come down in." He doesn't mean drive until you come to the end of the rainbow, or all you'll get is a shot of that pot of gold. Just drive until you can find a gorge, or a water source, or something—anything interesting—for it to end with. Do those two things and you'll wind up with a remarkable shot.

Removing Distracting Junk

SCOTT KELBY

In some of my landscape photo workshops, we do a class critique of shots from the participants in the workshop (the person who took the image always remains anonymous during the critique, unless we all really love the shot, then they usually stand up and shout, "Hey, I took that!"). Anyway, one thing that always stands out as a spoiler of some otherwise great images is that the image has a distracting element (also known as "some distracting junk") in the photo. It can be a road sign, a sign on the beach (as you see above), an empty beer can, some telephone wires, or even a tree branch extending into the photo, and I've always felt if it doesn't add to the photo, it takes away from it. There are three different ways you can deal with this "junk" that creeps into your photos: (1) Compose around it. When you're shooting, be very aware of what's in your shot, especially in the background. Check all four sides of the frame (top, left side, right side, and bottom) for anything that you'll wish later wasn't there, and if you see something, change your composition to eliminate it. (2) Physically remove the distracting element (as long as you're not a photojournalist). If there's a beer can, a twig, some trash, etc., pick it up and move it out of the frame (be careful not to damage anything in nature—period!). Or, (3) remove it later in Adobe Photoshop using either the Healing Brush tool, Patch tool, or the Clone Stamp tool. I've done a quick video clip for readers of this book to show you how to use these three tools, and you can watch it at www.kelbytraining.com/books/digphotogv2.

Where to Focus for Landscape Shots

SCOTT KELBY

When you're taking a landscape shot, where do you focus your camera's focal point (that red dot in the center of your viewfinder. Well, its default spot is in the center, but you can move that spot, so if you moved yours, get it back to the middle for this)? With landscape shots, the rule is: you want to focus about one-third of the way into the image. This gives you the widest possible range of focus throughout the image. Also, another trick you can use is to shoot big, sweeping landscape shots at f/22, which gives you the most focus from front to back in your shot.

Getting the Clearest Landscapes Possible

Have you ever seen a landscape photo that just has incredible clarity throughout the image? I'm not talking about sharpness—I'm talking clarity (like a total lack of haze, or fog, or any other atmospheric effect). Well, there's a technique for getting that amazing clarity, and it's simple: shoot in winter. The air is the clearest during winter time, and it's the perfect time of year to get those amazingly clear shots that you just can't get any other time of year.

Find the Great Light First

SCOTT KELBY

A few years ago, my friend, and landscape photography hero, Bill Fortney said some-thing that really had an impact on my photography and I'm going to pass it on to you. Bill feels that the single most important thing in a shot of any kind is the quality of light, and that the quality of light is so important that he'll search for great light first, and then once he finds that great light, he'll find a subject—something or somebody to shoot in that wonderful light. Essentially, if the light is great, you'll find a subject, but if you've found a great subject, you have to be very, very lucky for great light to just magically appear. In short: "It's all about the light." Once you get that, everything else falls into place. It's deeper than it sounds.

How to Shoot on a Gray, Overcast Day

SCOTT KELBY

This one might sound kind of obvious when I say it, but I can't tell you how many times I've been out shooting with a group and one or more people in the group has come up and said, "Well, the sky is totally messing up our shoot today." While a gray sky definitely stinks, there is something you can employ for shooting on gray-sky days, and that is simply to compose so little (or none) of that gray sky winds up in your shots. If you go into the shoot knowing that you're going to do your best to avoid seeing the sky in any of your shots, you can then get all of the benefits that a gray sky usually brings, which are colors that are actually fairly saturated and softer shadows throughout your images. You probably won't be able to fully eliminate the sky from your photos, so just compose your shots so the amount of sky you do see is kept to a minimum. This simple technique has saved many a shoot.

A Trick for Great-Looking Flower Shots

SCOTT KELBY

Want a great quick trick for some interesting-looking flower shots? Get down low, and shoot the flowers so they're backlit, with the sun behind them. The sunlight shining through the translucent petals creates a beautiful effect, and this is a popular trick employed by serious flower shooters that works every time. Don't forget to get down low (so low that you're either shooting straight on or up at the flowers) to get the most from this effect.

The Full-Frame Camera Advantage

The vast majority of today's digital cameras have a built-in magnification factor because of the size of the sensors in the camera. For example, most Nikon cameras have a 1.4x magnification factor, and what that means is if you put a 100mm lens on a Nikon digital camera (like a D40, D50, D70, D80, D200, D2x), that 100mm lens becomes a 140mm lens because of the sensor's magnification factor. Most Canon cameras have a 1.6x magnification (like the Digital Rebel, Digital Rebel XTi, 20D, 30D, and 40D), which makes a 200mm lens more like a 320mm lens. Many sports shooters, birders, and a host of other photographers who routinely use zoom and telephoto lenses love this added reach from digital sensors, but when it comes to the wide-angle lenses landscape photographers use, it can somewhat work against us. For example, a 12mm wide-angle Nikon lens becomes a less-wide 16mm lens. For Canon shooters, a 14mm wide-angle lens becomes a 22mm equivalent. That's why some landscape photographers are drooling over the new full-frame digital cameras, like Nikon's D3 or Canon's 5D (shown above), both of which are full-frame, and when you put a 12mm on the Nikon, it's that same, beautifully wide 12mm aspect ratio we used to enjoy back in the film days. When you put a 14mm on a Canon 5D, it's the same thing—a real 14mm with no extra magnification. I'm not saying you need to switch, or that you bought the wrong camera, I just want you to know what all the fuss is about for landscape photographers and other people who "go wide."

Chapter Five

Shooting Weddings Like a Pro

How to Get Professional Results from Your Next Shoot

Shooting a wedding is tricky business, and if you have friends (and they know you have a nice camera), it's only a matter of time before you're standing in a church yelling things like, "Okay, next I need the groom's grandmother and grandfather." Once you've said that line aloud in a church, you are officially ordained as a temporary wedding photographer. Now, just because you took the gig for free, as a favor to that guy you know over in accounting, don't think for a minute that the bride is expecting anything less than absolute pro-quality images. Worse yet, the nicer gear you have, the better they expect those images to be, and if, up until this day, you've been a sports shooter or a landscape photographer, all that goes out the window, because today you are a wedding photographer, which is arguably the single hardest photography job in the known world. The reason is simple: there is no reshoot. This particular wedding, the one you are responsible for shooting, only happens once. There is no, "Oh, my camera broke" or "I didn't bring enough memory cards" or "I forgot my charger for my flash," because if the bride hears anything even approaching one of those excuses, she will take her bare hands and squeeze your neck until either your lifeless body falls to the floor like a wet bag of cement, or a pack of AAA alkaline batteries pops out of you like a Pez dispenser. That's because regardless of whether you're getting paid or not, she has waited, dreamed about, meticulously planned, agonized over, and micro-managed this special day to death, and if you miss any one of those critical moments (the ring, kissing the bride, walking down the aisle as man and wife for the first time, cutting the cake, the first dance, etc.), then it's time for you to die. That's why this chapter is all about one thing: increasing your life expectancy.

Create a Shot List

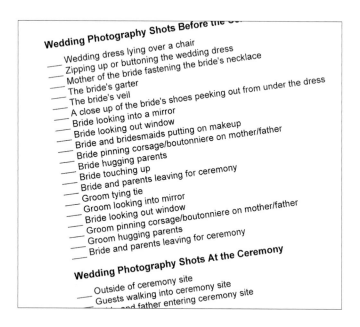

Wedding Photography Shots Before the ...
_____ Wedding dress lying over a chair
_____ Zipping up or buttoning the wedding dress
_____ Mother of the bride fastening the bride's necklace
_____ The bride's garter
_____ The bride's veil
_____ A close up of the bride's shoes peeking out from under the dress
_____ Bride looking into a mirror
_____ Bride looking out window
_____ Bride and bridesmaids putting on makeup
_____ Bride pinning corsage/boutonniere on mother/father
_____ Bride hugging parents
_____ Bride touching up
_____ Bride and parents leaving for ceremony
_____ Groom tying tie
_____ Groom looking into mirror
_____ Bride looking out window
_____ Groom pinning corsage/boutonniere on mother/father
_____ Groom hugging parents
_____ Bride and parents leaving for ceremony
Wedding Photography Shots At the Ceremony
_____ Outside of ceremony site
_____ Guests walking into ceremony site
_____ ... and father entering ceremony site

Before you even leave your office to head to the wedding, you should put together a shot list of photos you'll need to take for the wedding album, prints, etc. There are no redos at weddings, so you'd better be sure you leave with a list in hand of which shots you need, from bride and groom formals, to detail shots (the invitations, the rings, the bouquet, the bride's shoes, etc.), to reception shots like cutting the cake, receiving lines, place cards, and more. Without a written shot list, you're winging it, and it's almost an absolute lock that you'll miss one or more critical shots that your clients (the bride and groom) are going to expect to be in their album, so don't take a chance—this little bit of preparation can make a world of difference. Luckily, you can find wedding photography shot lists online for free at places like http://weddings .about.com/od/photographer/a/Photogchecklist.htm or this article and shot list from Amazon.com at www.amazon.com/b?ie=UTF8&node=13876911 (actually, there are literally hundreds of different shot lists available for downloading—just Google "wedding shot list" and you'll have a wide range of choices). Find a shot list that makes sense to you, and although you can get creative and do far beyond what it suggests, at least you'll have the most critical shots covered. Also, make sure you talk to the bride and groom before you finalize your shot list to ensure the specific shots they want are included (they may want shots with old friends from high school or college, or a special relative, and the only way to find out about these is to talk with the bride and groom in advance).

Have Backups for Everything!

Two
Camera
Bodies

Extra
Flash
Batteries

Extra
Camera
Batteries

Backup
Flash

If anything can go wrong at the wedding you're shooting, it will. That's why the pros always take backups for everything, because there are no retakes, no redos, no "do overs." Go through each piece of your gear and ask yourself what you would do if it wound up missing or broke. I can tell you this, at the very minimum you need to have two camera bodies—one main and one backup (a friend of mine was shooting a wedding, his camera slipped out of his hands, and the shoot was over. He was lucky enough to have a friend race him a replacement camera, but if his friend wasn't available, or was shooting a wedding himself that day, or was at the movies, etc., he probably would have wound up in court). You also need backup batteries for your flash, and even a backup flash unit. You need extra memory cards and a backup lens (I recently saw a photographer pick up his camera bag, which he thought was zipped, and we all cringed at the sound of breaking glass). Also, don't forget to bring backup batteries for both of your cameras. It comes down to this: you don't want to put yourself in a situation where one piece of equipment fails, one piece gets dropped, or your battery dies, and your job is in jeopardy (not to mention the loss of future wedding gigs from the fallout of having a large public event like a wedding day shoot go belly up).

Silencing Your Camera's Beep

The last thing the wedding couple (or the clergy, or the guests) wants to hear during the ceremony is the distracting sound of your camera beeping as it locks focus. Before the wedding begins, go to your camera's menu and disable the audible beep sound. From that point on, use the focus symbol that appears in your camera's viewfinder to let you know when the auto-focus has locked on. Once the ceremony is over, you can always switch back.

Backlighting Your Bride

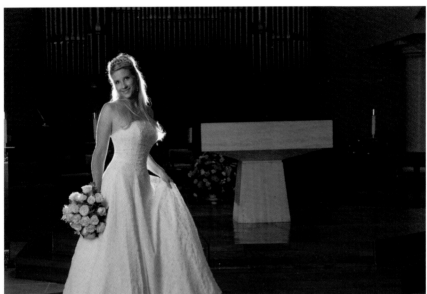

SCOTT KELBY

A popular effect with wedding photographers is to backlight the bride—where a bright light rims the outline of the bride—and then add in just a little bit of flash to light the front of the bride, so she's not a silhouette (as shown above). This takes two flash units: one in front of the bride (in this case, I used an off-camera flash on a light stand, positioned to the left of the camera at a 45° angle), and a second flash on a light stand directly behind the bride (so the bride's dress covers the light stand and flash). The flash of light from the front flash triggers the second flash behind the bride. The key is to make sure the flash behind the bride is much brighter than the flash in front of the bride (in the shot above, I lowered the power of the front flash as low as I could, but kept it bright enough so it would still trigger the flash behind her. It took a couple of test flashes to find out just how low that front flash could go). Another nice look (which is very dramatic) is to go ahead and let her just be lit with a flash behind her, then turn the flash in front off, so she actually is mostly a silhouette. If you do this, you'll have to set your flash so it doesn't fire the full flash, but only a very low light pulse—just enough to trigger the wireless flash behind her, but so it doesn't throw any measurable light on the bride (Nikon's dSLRs with pop-up flash have this feature built in).

Don't Changes Lenses, Change Cameras

DAVE CROSS

Once a wedding starts, things happen very quickly and you're not going to have a lot of chances (read as: none) to change lenses. So, if you're shooting with your zoom lens, and you suddenly need to switch to a wide angle, take a tip from professional sports shooters and don't switch lenses—switch camera bodies instead. That's right—keep two camera bodies around your neck (or one around your neck, one in your hand), and put a wide-angle lens on one body, and a zoom lens on the other. That way, switching lenses takes two seconds, not two minutes, and because of that, now you "get the shot."

Another Two-Camera Strategy

Besides the zoom and wide-angle double-camera technique above, here's another one to consider: have one camera with a flash mounted on your hot shoe for when you need flash, and have your second camera with a really fast lens, like a 50mm f/1.8 or f/1.4 (see page 137) for when you can't use flash (or don't want to use it), so you can capture those intimate moments without being obtrusive.

Bring a Stepladder for a Higher Vantage Point

At weddings, you're going to be posing and shooting large groups (for your formals), and one trick the pros use is to carry a small, lightweight, collapsible aluminum ladder, like the 3-step Franzus LadderKart, which doubles as a hand truck to help you move your gear (when you're not standing on it). It holds up to 300 lbs., and I've found it online for as low as $43 (Brookstone.com has a similar ladder/cart for $60). Being able to shoot the formal group portraits from a higher angle is a big help, because it enables you to see more faces and arrange your groups more easily. Also, it's great for shots during the reception, where a higher angle gives you a better view of the bride and groom on the crowded dance floor. Actually, you can put it to use anytime you want a different perspective, plus you can even use it as a posing stool in a pinch. You'll find this to be an indispensable tool (even if you only wind up using it for lugging your gear).

Why You Want a Second Shooter

RAFAEL "RC" CONCEPCION

Many pro wedding photographers bring a second shooter to their jobs (sometimes even a third shooter) as an insurance policy to make sure they cover all the most important shots, and the bigger the wedding, the more you need a second shooter. After all, you can't be everywhere, and if any little thing goes wrong (equipmentwise or otherwise), there's someone else to either keep shooting, or to deal with the problem so you can keep shooting. This second shooter also usually acts as an assistant, and in the fast pace of a wedding, this second shooter can be an absolute lifesaver, but beyond that—the second shooter may (will) have a different style than you and can bring a different dimension (they can shoot zoom while you're shooting wide), a different camera angle, they can shoot from a different location in the church and reception hall, plus there's a good chance that if you missed "the shot" your second shooter will have gotten it (or vice versa).

When to Shoot in RAW

Although many wedding photographers choose to shoot exclusively in JPEG mode, when you get in a tricky lighting situation, your Get Out of Jail Free card is to switch to RAW mode. Here's why: when you shoot in JPEG mode, the white balance you set in the camera is embedded into the file. If you set it wrong (which can happen in tricky lighting situations), you've got a color correction nightmare. However, when you shoot in RAW mode, you have the option of changing the white balance to any one of the same white balance settings you could have chosen in the camera itself. Best of all, once you've fixed the white balance for one photo, you can apply that change to all the other images at once. If you use Adobe Photoshop CS2 or CS3, here's how: (1) Select all the RAW photos you want to adjust and open them in Photoshop's Camera Raw (it will open all your selected photos at once). (2) Choose the White Balance setting from the pop-up menu. (3) Click the Select All button at the top left. (4) Click the Synchronize button, and when the dialog appears, choose White Balance from the pop-up menu at the top, then click OK. Now the white balance you chose for the current RAW photo will be applied to all your other open RAW photos. If you use Adobe Lightroom, select the photos you want to adjust, then go to the Develop module and choose your new white balance. Click the Copy button on the bottom left. When the dialog appears, click the Check None button, turn on just the checkbox for White Balance, then click Copy. Now click the Paste button to paste that white balance setting to all your other selected photos. Also, if you want the best of both worlds, set your camera to Raw + JPEG, which captures a RAW image and a JPEG version at the same time.

Where to Aim Your Flash

DAVE CROSS

Another one of the tricks the pros use to get just that little extra bit of light into their wedding photos (even ones taken in daylight) is to aim their flash head straight upward (as shown here). This works best if you're not standing too far from your subjects, and even if there's no ceiling to bounce the light from the flash off of, it still sends that little bit of light forward to light the face. This helps in adding catch lights in the eyes, but it does it without creating that "too much flash" look. To help make sure those catch lights appear, pull up your flash's bounce card to help direct more of that straight-up light forward (you can see the white bounce card pulled up in the photo above). So, if you've got a nice white ceiling to let the light from your flash bounce off of—great (but keep that bounce card extended either way). If not, still keep that flash aimed straight up most of the time, especially if there's already some existing room light, as the light from your flash will be subtle enough to nicely blend in.

Shoot in Lower Light Without Raising Your ISO

Since you'll be shooting on a regular basis in the low lighting of a church, there's a tool many of the top pros use that lets them get away with shooting perfectly exposed, sharp, handheld shots without using flash, or without pumping their ISO up to 1200. They buy an inexpensive 50mm f/1.8 lens (right around $100), or better yet, a 50mm f/1.4 lens (like the one shown above, which goes for around $285). These super-fast lenses let you shoot handheld in really low light, and you won't find a wedding pro that has one who doesn't swear by it. They're lightweight, surprisingly crisp (considering their low cost), and another tool in your bag of tricks to make sure you get the most important shots.

A Recipe for Balanced Flash in Church

SCOTT KELBY

When you're shooting the formals in the church (before or after the ceremony), here is a recipe you can use to get a natural-looking light balance between your flash and the available light in the church: set your ISO to 800, set your shutter speed to 1/60 of a second, and set your f-stop to f/5.6, or a lower number if possible (like f/4, f/3.5, or even f/2.8). By using a relatively low shutter speed like 1/60 of a second, it's a slow enough speed that your camera can properly expose the background (you see it lit with the available light in the room), and then your flash comes in to freeze the action. Once you've got those two settings in place, now all you have to do is take a test shot with your flash, and if it overpowers the room light (the background looks black), then lower the brightness (power) of your flash unit, so although your subject will be mostly lit with flash, you'll still see some of the natural light in the church. This gives a nice balance between the natural light (which should be around 30% to 35% of the light in the photo) and your flash (which should be 60% to 65% of the light).

Compose to Include the Church

This is one of many tricks I learned from my friend, and wedding photography guru, David Ziser (a master wedding photographer and brilliant teacher): compose a decent number of the formal bride and groom portraits to include a lot of the interior of the church (as shown above). It's important to brides to see the church where the ceremony took place, and by composing it into the formals, it really gives the shots a sense of place (after all, if you compose them so tight that you don't see the church, you might as well have taken them the day before in the studio).

Don't Forget Your Business Cards

There is no better place to book new business than at the wedding you're shooting, and if you seem calm, in control, and confident, you may get inquiries right there on the spot (before your prospective client has even seen a single image). They assume if you got this gig, you must be good, so make sure you have some extra business cards on you. Writing your number on a napkin doesn't instill confidence.

Add B&W to the Album

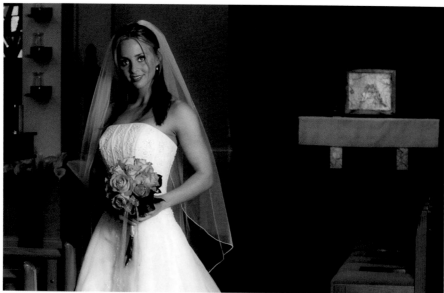

SCOTT KELBY

Another popular element in today's wedding albums is to include a number of black-and-white images. You'll still shoot these in color, and then you'll use Adobe Photoshop to convert some of your images into black and white. This enhances the "photojournalistic" look of the wedding album, it adds contrast to the album, and many wedding photos look just wonderful in black and white. If you have Photoshop CS3, there is a new Black & White conversion tool that does a pretty decent job of converting your color image into black and white (and it comes with some built-in presets—you just have to choose one you like). If you have Photoshop CS2 or Photoshop Elements, they can do the job, as well. I've created a short video clip to show you how to convert from color to black and white in Photoshop CS3, CS2, and Elements—you can find it on this book's download site at www.kelbytraining.com/books/digphotogv2.

Charge Everything the Day Before the Wedding

The day before the wedding, make sure you charge everything—including your cameras (both bodies). Make sure you have fresh batteries in all your flash units. If you're taking your laptop, make sure its batteries are charged. And just make certain that if a piece of your equipment has a battery, it's a fresh battery, or a freshly charged battery. Also, it's not a bad idea to fill your car up with gas now, too.

The Advantage of a Flash Bracket

DAVE CROSS

Another popular tool with wedding photographers is a flash bracket. These brackets get the flash off the camera and up high enough away from the lens that they nearly eliminate the red-eye problem caused by flash. But there's another huge advantage that becomes clear the moment you go to shoot a shot in vertical (portrait) orientation. If your flash is sitting on top of your camera (in the flash hot shoe), and you turn the camera sideways for a tall shot, your flash winds up lying on its side to the side of your camera, so now you have a new set of problems. Well, a flash bracket lets you flip the flash back upright, so although the camera is turned sideways, the flash is still straight above your lens. The flash bracket I use is the WPF-1 Wedding Pro Flash Bracket from Really Right Stuff (it's $150 direct from www.reallyrightstuff.com). It's extremely well-built, lightweight, and it lets you flip your flash upright with just one simple move. (*Note:* When using a flash bracket, I always use a dome diffuser to soften and spread the light, and still try to bounce the light off the ceiling or nearby wall whenever possible. At the very least, I aim the flash straight upward as mentioned in "Where to Aim the Flash" a couple pages back.)

Tip for Posing the Bride

SCOTT KELBY

Another tip I picked up from David Ziser is a posing tip for formal shots of the bride that lowers the shoulder that's farthest from your light source, which creates a flattering diagonal line between her shoulders. To do this, have the bride stand with her feet in a staggered V-shape (as shown above), and then have her shift her weight to her back foot, which creates a much more dynamic look for your pose.

Dealing with the "Unofficial" Wedding Shooters

When you're hired as the official wedding photographer, these days you're probably going to have to deal with a number of "unofficial" photographers (friends of the bride/groom with digital SLRs) who want to shoot over your shoulder while you're doing the formals. Well-known photographer and author Derrick Story shared a tip with me that might help give you some breathing room so you can get your job done. Derrick goes over to the unofficial shooters and asks that they let him get his job done first, then he'll hold the group in place for a few a moments so they can step in and get their shots. He finds that this usually does the trick, and they stay out of his hair while he's getting the formals taken care of.

Keeping Detail in the Bridal Gown

Since most bridal gowns are white, we have to be careful how we position the bride when shooting the formal bridal portraits, so we don't blow out the highlights on the gown and lose all the important detail of the dress (and that detail is *very* important to the bride). David Ziser taught me a great trick that works every time for keeping this critical detail, and it has to do with how you position the bride. You want the light from your flash (or from a window, if you're using window light) to cross the dress (so it accentuates the shadows and brings out detail), not hit it straight on and blow everything out. The easiest way to do this is simply to position your bride so her shoulder that is closest to the light source is angled toward the light source. That's it. This is important because if the shoulder closest to the light isn't in front, the flash hits the gown straight on and you lose the shadows and the detail. So, just make sure to angle the bride so her shoulder that's closest to the light is angled toward the light (as shown here, where you can see by looking at the bride, the flash is to the left of my camera, because she's much brighter on that side. The shoulder closest to the camera is aiming toward the light). Easy enough.

Getting More Flashes Per Wedding

Your flash is going to get a workout at a wedding, and you're going to be stopping to pop in fresh batteries on a pretty regular basis. Batteries must sense fear, because they always seem to die during absolutely critical moments in the wedding, so you want to be changing batteries as little as possible. (Plus, as your batteries start to wear down, it starts to take longer and longer for your flash to recycle so it's ready to fire again.) That's why many pros use a small external battery pack to double how long they can shoot with flash before having to change batteries. Better yet, it greatly cuts the recycle time between flashes. These packs are a little larger than a deck of cards, and run on six or eight AA batteries (depending on the model). You just connect the pack's cable to your flash, pop the pack into your shirt or suit pocket, and fire away. If you don't have a battery pack and your battery's getting low, try shooting at a higher ISO—it cuts the flash output and extends your battery life considerably.

Scott's Gear Finder

Nikon SD-8A High Performance Battery Pack (around $140)

Canon Compact Battery Pack CP-E4 (around $150)

Quantum Slim & Compact Turbo Battery Packs (around $425 and up)

How to Lessen Noise in Your Photos

When you raise the ISO on your camera (so you can shoot in lower light), there is a tradeoff, and that is you increase the amount of noise (grain) in your shots. Depending on the make and model of your camera, this noise might be acceptable or it might be so visible that it kind of ruins the shot. However, I've found an inexpensive, easy-to-use Photoshop plug-in that does a brilliant job of removing high ISO noise from wedding photos, while maintaining as much of the important detail in the photo as possible. It's called Noiseware Professional (from www.imagenomic.com for $69.95), and it does a brilliant job of removing this type of noise (I just use the presets it comes with, rather than messing with the sliders and other controls. In fact, I've never used anything but the built-in presets). But beyond just removing noise, a happy side effect is that it usually also softens your bride's (and bridesmaids') skin. So, it removes noise and softens skin. What's not to like? (Two other popular noise plug-ins are Noise Ninja and Dfine 2.0.)

A Tip for Outdoor Weddings

If you go a day early to scope out the location where you'll be shooting an out-door wedding, make sure you're there at the exact same time of day that you'll be actually shooting the wedding. That way, you can see what the real lighting conditions will be when you're shooting the "real thing."

Tips for Shooting the Bride's Profile

Here are a few more tips I picked up from David Ziser for making perfect profile portraits of your bride: (1) Shoot horizontal. As I mentioned in the portrait chapter, this puts some breathing room in front of your subject, so they don't look squeezed into the frame. (2) Position the bride so it's a full profile shot, where you don't see any of the eye on the other side of her head, or any of the other side of her face at all. (3) Don't position your flash (or softbox) directly in front of her face—position it slightly behind her so the light wraps around her face. (4) Don't have her look straight ahead, or you'll see too much of the whites of her eyes. Instead, have her look just a tiny bit back toward the camera (don't let her move her head—just her eyes). That way, you see more iris and less whites. (5) If the shadow side of her face (the side facing the camera) gets too dark, use a silver reflector to bounce some of that light into that dark side of her face.

Get to the Church Early and Scope Everything Out

The last thing you want during the wedding shoot is to frantically search for good light, good backgrounds to shoot in front of, or a power outlet to plug in your charger. Get there crazy early (or go a day before the wedding, if possible) and scope everything out in advance. That way, you're calm, prepared, and you have some great spots already picked out so the couple looks their best.

Wedding Zoom Effect Made Easy

SCOTT KELBY

Here's a popular effect for adding a sense of motion and energy to your reception shots (perfect for dance floor shots). It's a zoom effect that you create using your flash and zoom lens, and it's easier to get than it looks. First, set your camera to manual mode, and lower your shutter speed to around 1/8 of a second (or slower). Then, zoom in tight on the couple dancing, press the shutter button with your right hand, and then immediately zoom the lens out all the way to wide angle with your other hand. Because the shutter is open while you're moving the zoom lens, it creates that motion effect, and then your flash fires to freeze the motion. The key is to zoom out to wide just as soon as you press that shutter button. Try this just a few times and you'll "get it." (That's another benefit of digital photography—you can try the trick and look at the LCD on the back of your camera to see if you got the zoom effect or not. If you didn't, you can just try again.)

Throw Some Snacks in Your Camera Bag

While everybody else is eating, you're expected to be shooting, so make sure you throw a few small snacks (energy bars are ideal) and some bottled water in with your gear. Even if the bride and groom have offered to feed you while you're there, you probably won't get a chance (once a reception starts, there's no break—too much is happening), so keep some snacks and water handy.

Read David Ziser's *Digital ProTalk* Blog Daily

If you're serious about this stuff, do what I do: read David Ziser's *Digital ProTalk* blog every day. He is an absolute fountain of information for professional wedding photographers, and on his blog, he not only shares his tricks of the trade, and hard-earned techniques, he also shares some of his amazing photography (including some wonderful non-wedding imagery). Plus, David does a lot of live speaking gigs, and if you ever get to see him in person, he will just blow you away. David speaks for me each year at the Photoshop World Conference & Expo, and the first time I sat in on his class (which was an on-location wedding shoot at a local church, complete with professional bride and groom models), I was amazed. When I came back to the conference hall, one of my buddies asked me how his workshop was, and I described it this way: "He was teaching more than just lighting and posing. He was teaching them the business of today's wedding photography, in such a meaningful and straight-to-the-point way that it was like he was running around stuffing money in their pockets. It was that good!" I find his blog as inspirational as it is informative. Check it out at www.digitalprotalk.com.

Chapter Six

Shooting Travel Like a Pro

How to Bring Back Photos That Really Make Them Wish They Were There

When you come home from a really amazing trip, it's not enough to chronicle your trip through photos and show factual images that detail where you were. You want to move people. You want to create images that are so powerful that they make the person viewing them want to go there so badly that they're willing to risk a series of white collar crimes (mostly embezzling) to pay for their trip to that very same place. Now, if you took good enough shots, it won't be long before your friends are overcome with emotion (jealousy) and will have to go to the exact same location to experience that same amazing feeling once again. Now, if either of your two friends have dSLR cameras, it's helpful to understand right up front that they're not going to that spot because they trust your judgment on travel. They're going there because they think they can get better photos from that spot than you did. Then, once they come back and show off their images, all your mutual friends will say something like, "Did you see Rick's photos from Machu Picchu? Wow, his were much better than Sandy's" and at that moment—you've been blinged. Actually, this is what is known as an IB, or an "Intentional Bling," and it gives you some insight into just how shallow your friends really are. But as shallow as they are, you can drain a little more water out of the pond by pulling this quick and easy stunt: when they see a really cool travel shot of yours, and they ask you where you took it (which means they don't already recognize the landmark)—lie. They'll never know. For example, if you shot the Portland Head lighthouse in Cape Elizabeth, Maine, tell 'em it's the Nauset lighthouse in North Eastham, Massachusetts. By the time they catch on, they'll already be back home, and you can feign a mysterious illness.

In This Case, Less Gear Is More

I'm a total gear freak, but the one time I definitely don't want to lug around a lot of gear is when I'm doing travel photography. You're going to be lugging your gear all day long, hopping on and off of all sorts of transportation, and as the day goes on, your gear seems to get heavier and bulkier, and by the end of the day, you've all but stopped digging around in your camera bag. To get around that, take as little with you as possible—one or two lenses, tops. For example, Nikon makes a reasonably priced 18–200mm lens with built-in VR (vibration reduction; as shown above) that lets you leave your camera bag back in the hotel because you've got everything covered from wide angle to long telephoto in just one lens. Canon makes an affordable 28–200mm lens that doesn't go quite as wide as the Nikon, but is amazingly small and lightweight. Also, there are some incredibly lightweight travel tripods available today, ranging from the Slik Sprint Pro for around $80 to what is probably the best travel tripod on the planet, the Gitzo GT1550T Traveler carbon-fiber tripod (for around $650). When it comes to lugging around lots of gear in an unfamiliar city, travel photography is definitely a case of "less is more." Do yourself a favor and travel light—you'll find yourself taking more shots, because you're changing lenses and messing with your equipment less.

Working People into Your Travel Shots

©ISTOCKPHOTO/MARK VAN

If you want to improve your travel photos, here's a simple trick: add more people to your shots. When you really want to capture the flavor of an area, don't just shoot build-ings, cathedrals, and monuments—show the people of that area. Nothing conveys the character and soul of a city more than its people, and that's why so many of the top travel photo pros work people into the majority of their shots. The next time you're feeling disappointed with your travel shots, it's probably because you're looking at cold buildings and empty streets. Add people and everything changes (for the better).

How to Know What to Shoot

Before you travel to a new city, do some research to see what other photogra-phers have shot there and where they shot it from. One great place to do this type of research is the websites of the big stock agencies (like Corbis or Getty Images), where you can do a search for the country or city you're going to. You'll see some amazing images, and you'll get lots of ideas for how the pros cover that area.

Getting People to Pose

©ISTOCKPHOTO/PEETER VIISIMAA

Candid shots of some of the locals make a nice addition to your travel shots, but if you have too many of them, they start to look less like travel photos and more like surveillance photos. To get those close-up, fascinating personal shots, you'll need to get some of the locals to pose for you. One of the best tricks for getting people to stop what they're doing and pose for you is to get them to let you take the first shot. When they see that I have a camera, I smile at them, hold up the camera with my finger on the shutter, and nod my head as if to say, "Is it okay if I take your picture?" Most of the time, they smile and nod back, and pause just long enough to let me snap one photo. Then I immediately turn the camera around and show them the photo on the camera's LCD monitor. Once they see that photo on your LCD, it kind of breaks down a barrier, because everybody loves a photo (especially if they're the subject), and they're usually more than happy to pose for a few more.

A Surefire Way to Get Them to Pose (Buy Stuff)

If you're uncomfortable with the "lift-and-nod" technique I outlined above, here's one that can't miss—find somebody selling something and buy one. If you're in a market, and you buy something from a vendor, you can bet that they'll pose for a quick picture or two, because now you're not just some tourist with a camera, you're one of their customers. This one works like a charm.

What to Shoot on Overcast Days

SCOTT KELBY

When the weather gets cloudy and overcast, don't pack up your gear—this is the time to shoot people on the street, open-air markets, stained glass windows (which look great under cloudy skies), and close-ups of architecture (as long as you do your best to avoid including any of that gray, cloudy sky). Cobblestone streets are great to shoot right after it has rained, and flowers photograph great under the shade that comes from a cloudy sky. Plus, if the sky gets really nasty, it may be a great time to shoot the sky itself. If it's just a flat gray, it's boring. But if a storm is on the way, the dark clouds can make an interesting subject, or add to a boring subject just with the shadows and mystery they bring.

What to Do If Your Room Doesn't Have a View

If you can't get a room with a view (see next page), try these: (1) See if there's a restaurant or lounge at the top of the hotel—you can bet it has plenty of great views, and they may let you shoot there at dusk, before they start serving dinner. (2) See if you can take a few shots from the rooftop. Strike up a rapport with the concierge (give him a big tip) and you'll be amazed at the doors that will open.

Shooting from Your Hotel Room

SCOTT KELBY

Everybody wants to have a "room with a view," and now you have even more motiva-
tion to ask for just that, because your hotel room can be a wonderful platform to shoot
the city from. When you check in, ask for a room on the highest available floor and be
prepared for some amazing opportunities to unfold right outside your window. If you
don't have a balcony, or a window you can open, you can shoot right through the window if you follow these three rules: (1) Turn off any lights in your hotel room—they'll
cause reflections in the glass that can show up in your photos—and (2) put your lens
as close to the glass as possible (I keep a lens hood on my lenses, so I put the lens hood
right on the glass itself. If you think you'll be doing this a lot, you can buy a rubber lens
hood, which runs from around $5 on up). And, (3) you can often use a polarizing filter
to cut the reflections in the glass, but since you lose some light, you might need to
shoot on a tripod, which makes getting right against the glass that much trickier. (I'm
not even going to count this last one as a rule, because I hope it goes without saying,
but…don't use your flash.)

The Magic Time for Cityscapes

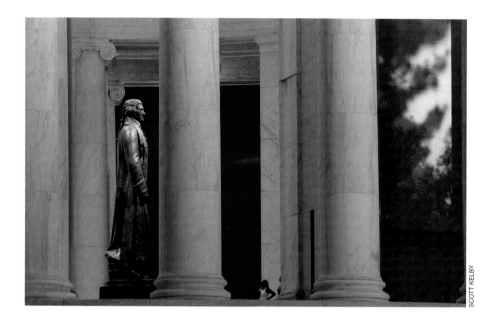

SCOTT KELBY

Great shots of cityscapes don't happen at 2:00 in the afternoon. If you want that killer shot of the city skyline, wait until about 30 minutes after sunset and shoot at twilight. The sky will usually be a rich, dark blue and the lights of the city will all be on, creating that magical photographic combination that creates the type of cityscapes you've always dreamed of taking. Now that you know what time to shoot, there's one more key to making this type of shot work, and that is you absolutely, positively must take this type of low-light shot with a tripod. Your shutter is going to have to stay open for a full second or more, and if you're not on a tripod, you're going to wind up with a blurry mess.

Taking the Cityscape Lights Shot Up a Notch

If the city you're shooting is near water, try to position yourself so that water comes between you and the city (for example, try shooting from a bridge). That way, you see reflections of the city lights in the water, which can add a tremendous amount of visual interest. This is another one of those "can't miss" travel shots, and what an impact it makes when friends, family, and even other photographers see your city-at-twilight-reflected-in-the-water shot.

Get These Shots Out of the Way First

SCOTT KELBY

If you travel to a famous city, your friends and family back home will be expecting shots of that city's most famous landmarks. For example, if you go to Paris, you'd better come back with some Eiffel Tower shots (cliché as they may seem), because people expect it. If you don't come back with some Eiffel tower shots, they'll be so distracted by what you didn't shoot that they won't pay attention to what you did shoot. So, get those out of the way first—shoot those ones for the folks back home now and get them "in the bag." That way, you can spend the rest of your time showing the city your way—shooting the people, the local flavor, the customs, and taking shots that speak to the photographer in you. One more thing: When you get back home, and friends and relatives tell you some of your shots look like postcards (and they will), just smile and thank them. Although photographers sometimes tend to look down on travel postcards, your average person doesn't, so if they tell you your shots "look like post-cards," they're actually paying you a huge compliment.

Shooting Famous Landmarks

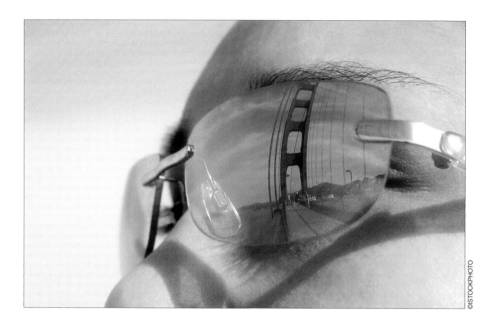

©ISTOCKPHOTO

If you're shooting a famous landmark, you can be sure it has already been shot a million times before, so it's incredibly hard to come back with a photo that hasn't been seen a million times (it's not impossible, just really hard). Here are a couple of ideas that might help you bring a fresh look to a landmark that has been shot to death: (1) Don't make the landmark the subject of your shot. For example, one of my favorite photos of Paris was taken by photographer Doug Merriam, and I love it because the subject is a French couple strolling along, holding hands, but the Eiffel Tower is clearly visible in the background. So, even though you can clearly see the landmark, it's not the subject, and that really made an impact with me. (2) Try showing the landmark as a reflection in water, or in a store window (picture the window of a Paris bistro with the Eiffel Tower reflecting in it), or the Arc de Triomphe reflecting in the chrome bumper of a French car, or better yet—in its side or rear view mirror. (3) Show only a small part of the landmark—just enough that it suggests the whole. The photo that I've taken of the Eiffel Tower that I like the best was taken 20 years ago (on Ektachrome 64 slide film), and it's of a nearby apartment building with one of the massive legs of the Eiffel Tower rising up behind it. You can't see anything but that one leg in the background, but you know it's the Eiffel Tower. It hung framed in my office for years.

Air Travel with Photo Gear

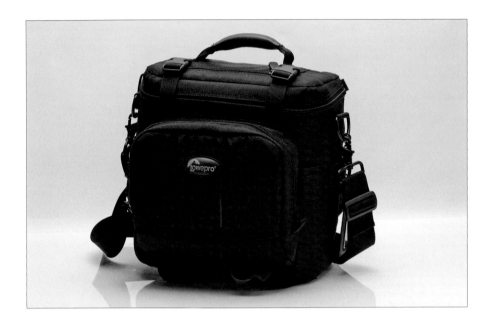

Earlier, I mentioned that you want to travel with as little gear as possible, and here's another reason—you absolutely, positively want to bring your gear on the plane as a carry-on. If your camera bag is too big and bulky, there's a good chance it won't fit in the overhead bin, especially if at some point in your trip you wind up in a smaller regional jet or turboprop with little, if any, overhead space. If you're thinking of buying a hard case and checking your gear, I'd reconsider. A photographer I know recently got *all* his checked gear stolen—lenses, camera bodies, flashes, the works! When he arrived at his destination and opened his case, it was completely empty. Keep your gear down to a minimum, take a small camera bag, and take it with you on the plane as a carry-on, and you'll avoid a lot of stress and complications, and possibly having to replace all of your gear.

Bring Extra Batteries

When you're in an unfamiliar city, the last thing you want to waste your time doing is searching for batteries (believe me, I learned this one the hard way), so make sure one thing you do bring with you is plenty of extra batteries for your flash unit and your camera (at the very least, recharge your camera battery every single night, because if your battery runs out, that's the end of the shoot).

Shoot the Food

SCOTT KELBY

Take a look at any great travel magazine and in every feature about a charming city, you'll always find a photo of its food. Trying new dishes is one of the most fun things about traveling to a new destination, so why wouldn't you include it in your photographs? Watch the expressions of people who look at your album when they come across a photo of a great-looking dish—do that once, and you'll always "shoot the food." Your best opportunities will be during the day, especially if you ask to sit near a window (to catch some of that gorgeous natural window light) or outside (preferably under an umbrella or awning, so you can shoot in shade). If you've got a white tablecloth (which is likely), you've got a great background to shoot on—just remove distracting items from around the dish as much as possible. Also, the classic food shots you see in these magazines generally have two things in common: (1) They generally use a very shallow depth of field (where the front of the plate is in focus and the back is somewhat out of focus). To get this effect, use the lowest f-stop possible (f/4, f/2.8, or even lower if you can). And, (2) shoot plates that have great presentation (in other words, shoot food that's beautifully arranged on the plate, which usually comes from higher-end restaurants). Desserts often are presented nicely, as are appetizers and sushi, and keep an eye out for anything served in a unique-looking dish.

Get a GPS for Your Digital Camera

COURTESY OF SONY

Today, you can buy small, incredibly lightweight GPS units that sit in your camera's hot shoe, and each time you take a photo, they embed the exact location (longitude and latitude) of where the shot was taken directly into the digital photo itself. Then, applications like Adobe Photoshop Lightroom can display that information (it appears in Lightroom's Metadata panel), and you're then one click away from seeing that location plotted on a Google map, and better yet, you can even see a satellite photo of that exact location while you're there. Sony makes a tiny GPS unit called the GPS-CS1KA that works with most digital cameras and the street price is around $120.

Have Someone Else Shoot You

If you're the one behind the camera, nobody's getting any shots of you in these fascinating, exotic, wonderful places. That's why you need to make it a point to get a friend or acquaintance you meet in your travels (even if it winds up being the waiter who serves you at a restaurant) to get at least a few shots of you. Although it might not mean much to you that you're not in any of your photos, it does mean something to your family and friends that you are in the shots.

Shooting Where They Don't Allow Flash

If you plan on shooting in museums, cathedrals, and other places that generally don't allow you to set up a tripod or use your flash, then I recommend buying an inexpensive 50mm f/1.8 lens. This is an old trick pro wedding photographers use (see the wedding photography chapter), and these super-fast lenses let in so much light that you can handhold shots where others dare not tread. Both the Nikon and Canon 50mm f/1.8 lenses sell for around $100 each, they take up little room in your camera bag, and they add very little weight to your bag, as well. If you can spring for an even faster lens (like an f/1.4, shown above, or an f/1.2), they let in an amazing amount of light, so you can fire away in incredibly low light (like candlelight situations) without having to raise your camera's ISO to 800 or more (which can greatly increase the amount of noise in your images).

When They Won't Let You Set Up Your Tripod

If you're in a place where they just won't let you set up your tripod, but the light is so low that your camera is going to leave the shutter open for a few seconds, try using your camera bag as a tripod. Turn your camera bag on its side, position it on a ledge, a counter, or any tall surface, then rest your camera on top. Put some spare batteries under the lens to support it and use the self-timer to take the shot.

Look for High Vantage Points

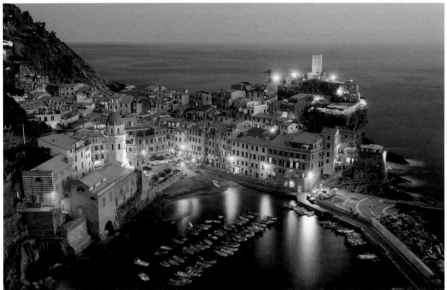

©ISTOCKPHOTO/BILL GROVE

Your average person's view of a city is going to be from the city streets (or from a tour bus on those streets), so if you want a more compelling place to shoot from, look for a different vantage point—one above the city. Look for towers, observation decks, tall hotels, church towers, cable cars, a bridge, an office building, or mountains overlooking the city, where you can show the city from a completely different view that your average photographer wouldn't get. It's just another thing that keeps your travel photos from looking average.

The Perfect Background Music for Travel Slide Shows

Want to find the perfect background music to put behind slides from your trip? Try this: buy the movie soundtrack from a movie that was filmed where you took your shots. For example, if your shots are from your trip to Italy, you can be sure you'll find instrumental background music that sounds very Italian in the movie *Under the Tuscan Sun*. If you shot in Paris, try the soundtrack from Disney's *Ratatouille*. If you shot in Russia, you can get some very dramatic Russian-sounding background music from the movie *The Sum of All Fears*. These all work so well because most movie scores are instrumental, which is ideal for your travel slide shows.

Give Yourself a Theme

Once you've shot the classic local landmark photos, here is a great way to spark your cre-ativity and show the city in a different light for a day: give yourself a mini-assignment. Pick a topic, spend part of the day focusing on that subject, and you'll be amazed at what you can come up with. For example, some of the mini–travel assignments I have given myself are: (1) shoot charming street numbers on the outsides of buildings, homes, and apartments; (2) shoot interesting doors and/or doorways; (3) shoot just things that are one vivid color; (4) shoot weather vanes; (5) shoot nothing but flowers; (6) shoot charming local barns; and (7) shoot close-ups of local architecture. Other ideas might be: shooting coffee cups; shooting those little food signs in local markets; shooting interesting columns, traffic signs or street signs, mailboxes, or things that are a particular shape (like only things that are round), or things of a particular color (only things that are red). You don't have to make one of these the only thing you do all day, just keep an eye out for it during your travels, and each time you see one of your as-signment objects, make sure you get it. Then, you can present these all together in one print (an example is shown above).

Chapter Seven

Shooting Macro Like a Pro

How to Take Really Captivating Close-Up Photos

If you're one of those people who believes life is all about the little details, then have I got a style of shooting for you. It's called macro photography (macro is actually an acronym that stands for Man, Are Cows Really Obnoxious), and it's based on a special type of lens called a macro or close-up lens, which lets you focus on objects much closer than you'd normally be able to, and because of this close-up capability, you can often get close enough so that your subject completely fills your frame. Some of the most popular subjects for macro-loving photographers to shoot are flowers, leaves, ladybugs on leaves, bees on flowers, and other everyday things in nature that we're not used to seeing close up. That's one of the things that makes macro photography so captivating: you're often seeing images at a view or magnification we rarely, if ever, see with the naked eye. Now, because I was just able to work the word "naked" into the book, it's almost guaranteed that the book will be a bestseller. That's because, from now on, anytime someone goes to the Web and searches for the word "naked" (so basically, most of my friends), one of the results they get back will be this book. Now, thinking that my book will have lots of nudie nakedness, these people will often buy it sight unseen, because apparently people who search for the word "naked" are also very loose with money—they'll buy any product that they feel will get them closer to actually seeing nudie nakedness. However, once they receive the book, they will soon realize, as you have (with great disappointment), that there is no nudie nakedness in the book, but if it makes you feel any better, I'm totally naked under my underwear (see that? I got the word "underwear" in now, too). Cha-ching!

Maximize Your Depth of Field

SCOTT KELBY

Macro lenses have a "sweet spot" where you get absolutely the most sharp results, and in macro photography, having tack-sharp images is critical. One trick to get the most sharpness out of your macro lens is to shoot with your lens aiming perfectly straight at the subject (in other words, don't angle your lens upward or downward toward your subject—try to shoot straight on for the best sharpness and clarity). So, for example, if you're shooting a bee on a flower, you'll need to lower your tripod to the point where you are aiming directly at the flower without having to tilt the lens, even a little bit (as shown above).

This Is Tripod Territory

Although there are now macro lenses that have built-in image stabilization (IS) or vibration reduction (VR), if you're serious about macro, you're going to be serious about how sharp your images are, which means you seriously need a tripod. This is absolutely tripod-land for sure, and a tripod may well be the single most important piece of your "making great macro shots" puzzle, so although you can cut a lot of corners in other areas, shooting on a tripod is one thing you absolutely, positively should do. They haven't yet come up with a built-in stabilization device that holds a camera as steady as even the cheapest tripod.

Why You Should Turn Auto-Focus Off

By now, you've learned that one of the big challenges of macro photography is getting things sharp and in focus. You're about to come to one of the things that can be the most frustrating, and this is using auto-focus when you're as close in on your subject as you are with macro shooting. If I can give you one tip that will lower your frustration level by a hundred, it's to turn off the auto-focus on your camera's lens and manually focus instead. I know, you hate to give up the auto-focus feature because, honestly, on today's cameras it's really amazingly accurate. That is, until you shoot macro. What will happen is your camera will try to find a focus point, and you'll hear the whirring of the lens as it tries to snap onto something, anything to focus on, and while it's getting frustrated—so are you. Just switch over to manual focus, and you'll both be better off.

Don't Touch That Shutter Button!

If you're going through the trouble of putting your camera on a tripod (and you absolutely should), you can still get a "less-than-tack-sharp" photo from the vibration that happens when you push the shutter button. That's why, when shooting macro, you should either use a shutter release cable (a cord that attaches to your camera that lets you take a shot without touching the shutter button on the camera itself) or use your camera's self-timer, which takes the shot for you about 10 seconds after you press the shutter button, so any vibration caused by your pressing the shutter button will be long gone.

Focus on the Eyes

In portrait photography, we always focus on the eyes to get the sharpest image. Same thing in wildlife photos. Same thing in macro shots of insects or butterflies, or any little critters that wind up in your viewfinder.

Which f-Stop Works Best

Is there an f-stop that works best for macro shots? Well, yeah. It's f/22. Because the depth of field of macro lenses is so shallow (meaning, the front of that flower you're shooting can be perfectly in focus and the petal just one inch behind it can be totally out of focus), you need to get as broad a depth as possible, and that comes when your aperture setting is at something like f/22. You could get away with f/16, or maybe even f/11, but to get the maximum amount of your subject in focus, try f/22 (or higher if your lens will allow). The higher the number, the more of your photo will be in focus.

Point-and-Shoot Macro Photography

Most compact point-and-shoot cameras these days actually have a macro lens built right into them—you just have to know how to engage it (so to speak). You do that by switching your mode dial to macro (its icon is usually a little flower, as shown circled above). This sets up your camera so you can get very close to your subject (like a flower, an insect, etc.) and still focus the camera (you can't get as close as you would with a dedicated macro lens on a dSLR, but you still can get surprisingly close for a compact digital camera). Once you've got this mode turned on, you can shoot using all the rest of the rules in this chapter, like shooting on a tripod, not shooting in even light wind, etc.

A Trick for Visualizing Macro

©ISTOCKPHOTO/CHRISTINE BALDERAS

When you're out shooting and you're looking at something and thinking, "I wonder if that would make a good macro shot?" you don't have to pull out all your gear and test it (especially because you probably won't). Instead, just carry a small magnifying glass (you can get thin plastic ones that fit in right in your wallet), then pull it out, go up to the object you're thinking about shooting, and you'll see right then and there whether it makes a good macro subject. Also, you can use this magnifier to try out different angles (think shooting flowers from way down low) before you go crawling around on your stomach with all your gear.

Simple Backgrounds Are Best

The same background rule we follow in portrait photography is also true in macro photography, and that is: keep the background simple. It may even be more important with macro than with portraits, because you're in so close your background will play a bigger role, so make sure your background is as simple as possible.

Why You Might Want to Shoot Indoors

A lot of nature macro photography is actually done indoors, rather than outside (in most cases, you're going to be so close in, you don't have to worry much about anyone realizing that you're in a studio). One of the main advantages of shooting macro indoors is that there's no wind. This might not seem like a big deal at first, but when you set up your camera with a macro lens outdoors and look through the lens, you'll see firsthand that the tiniest bit of wind—wind that you don't really even notice is there—is moving your flower (leaf, twig, etc.) all over your frame, which means your photos are going to be soft and out of focus. It'll really throw you, because you'll back away from the lens, and you'll swear there's no wind, but then you'll look through the viewfinder and know right away—you're hosed. Another advantage of shooting indoors is that you can control the light (especially if you're shooting under studio strobes), and the key to lighting macro shots is to have nice even lighting across the entire image. You don't want drama and shadows—you want nice even light, and getting that in the studio is easier than it is outdoors by a long shot.

Buying a Macro Lens

If this macro thing sounds really interesting, there are three ways you can dip your toe into the close-up shooting world: (1) Check to see if you already have a telephoto or zoom lens that has macro capability built right in. (2) Buy a macro lens—both Canon and Nikon make great macro lenses (that's a Canon lens above), and you can get a Sigma 105mm macro lens for around $399. And, (3) add a close-up lens attachment to one of your existing lenses. These screw on the end of your lens and turn any zoom lens into a macro lens (I have one of these, and it's small enough and lightweight enough that it goes with me everywhere I go). When it comes to macro lenses, the higher number the lens, the closer your subject will be in the frame (so a 65mm macro lens might get you the entire bee, but a 105mm will get so close you can get just the bee's head).

Create Your Own Water Drops

Use a tip from volume 1 of this book, and that is: don't wait for rain—bring a water bottle on your shoot and spray water on your flower petals (or leaves) to create the look of fresh raindrops, which look great in macro photography. Plus, if you get close enough, you'll be able to see reflections in the water drops themselves. Cool stuff.

Perfect, Even Light for Macro Shots

CHARLIE ENXUTO

When it comes to lighting close-up shots, your goal is to get as even lighting as possible, and there's actually a special flash, called a ring flash, that's designed to do exactly that. It's actually not one flash, it's a series of flashes attached to a ring that slides over your lens, and because these flashes light your subject from all sides, it creates that very even light you're looking for.

Scott's Gear Finder

Sigma EM-140 DG Macro Flash (around $360)

Canon MR-14EX Macro Ring Lite (around $450)

Nikon R1-C1 Wireless Close-Up Speedlight Flash w/SU-800 (around $625)

Making Your Lens into a Macro Lens

CHARLIE ENXUTO

The more space you put between your camera's sensor and your lens, the closer you'll be able to focus, and because of that, companies make extension tubes. These extension tubes attach between your lens and your camera (they look like a thin extra lens) to move the lens farther away from your camera's sensor, which cuts your minimum focus distance big time, so you can get in there and shoot nice and close (like you had a true macro lens). The advantage of these extension tubes is: they're much less expensive than a dedicated macro lens, starting around $75. (By the way, if you have a macro lens already, an extension tube can make your macro focus even closer. Sweet!)

SHUTTER SPEED: 1/20 SEC   F-STOP: F/11   ISO: 100   FOCAL LENGTH: 50mm   PHOTOGRAPHER: SCOTT KELBY

Chapter Eight

Pro Tips for Getting Better Photos

Tricks of the Trade for Making All Your Shots Look Better

There are some tricks of the trade that just don't fit under any of the existing chapters, because they're not really just about getting better-looking portraits or more luscious-looking landscapes—they're about being a better photographer and getting better shots. And getting better shots is what it's all about, right? This is something we're all very passionate about, and if we get to the point where we're actually starting to sell our work (maybe as fine art prints, or through assignment work with a magazine), and are turning our passion into profits, then we're really living the dream—doing something we truly love for a living. Speaking of dreams, I haven't made a big deal about this on my daily blog (www.scottkelby.com) or in any of my live classes yet, because I don't want it to come off like bragging, but I recently signed a year-long contract with *National Geographic* that I'm pretty psyched about. In the terms of this agreement, I get 12 monthly issues for only $15, which is 74% off the newsstand price, so as you might imagine, I'm very excited. Anyway, in this chapter, we're going to focus on lots of those little tricks of the trade that you can apply to a wide range of photography to make everything you shoot look that much better. Now, one last thing: You might have heard I run with a dangerous crowd. We ain't too pretty, we ain't too proud. We might be laughing a bit too loud, but that never hurt no one. (I just wanted to see if you're still reading this after that whole *National Geographic* scam I pulled on you above. Come on, you have to admit, I had you going there for just a second or two, didn't I?)

Which Mode to Shoot In

Not sure which mode you should be shooting in? Here are some tips:

Aperture Priority (Av): I recommend this mode for both portrait photographers and landscape photographers, because it gives you control over your background. You get to choose whether you want your background out of focus (by choosing lower numbered f-stops, like f/4 or f/2.8) or totally in focus (by choosing higher f-stop numbers, like f/11, f/16, and higher), and no matter your choice, your camera will automatically choose the right shutter speed to give you a good exposure.

Shutter Priority (S or Tv): I recommend this mode if you're shooting sports, where you generally need to freeze the action. This lets you choose to shoot with very high shutter speeds (provided you're shooting in bright enough light—like daylight), and then your camera will automatically choose the right f-stop for you to give you a good exposure.

Manual (M): If you're shooting with studio strobes, you need to shoot in manual mode, because in aperture priority or shutter priority, you won't get a proper exposure, as they won't take into account the fact that you're using strobes.

Program (P): Shoot in this mode when you want to be in point-and-shoot mode, but don't want the flash popping up. Perfect for when you need to quickly capture a moment and don't want to mess with any settings.

Choosing the Right ISO

Our goal is to shoot with our digital cameras set to the lowest possible ISO (ideally 100 ISO) for one simple reason—it offers the lowest amount of noise (grain) and gives us the sharpest, cleanest images possible. The only reason to raise your ISO is to be able to handhold your camera in low-light situations. So, for regular daylight or brightly lit situations, we shoot at 100 ISO. If you raise your camera's ISO setting to 200, it lets you handhold your camera in a little lower light and still get a sharp photo, but the trade-off is a tiny increase in visible noise. At 400 ISO, you can handhold in even lower light, but with more visible noise. At 800 ISO, you can handhold in the low light of a church, but with even more noise, and so on. It comes down to this: the higher the ISO, the lower light you can handhold your camera in, but the higher the ISO, the more noise you get, too. That's why we try to use tripods as much as possible. When our camera is on a tripod, it's perfectly still, so we can shoot at 100 ISO the whole time without worrying about getting blurry photos in low light.

Which Format to Shoot In (RAW, JPEG, or TIFF)

Most digital cameras these days (and all dSLRs) offer at least these three main file formats: RAW, JPEG, and TIFF. Here's when to use each:

JPEG: Shoot in JPEG if you're really good at nailing your exposure every time. If you're dead on (or really close) on your exposure and white balance, and don't think you'll need to tweak it much later (or at all) in Photoshop, then JPEG is for you. The file sizes are dramatically smaller, so you'll fit more on your memory card, and they'll take up less space on your computer.

RAW: Shoot in RAW mode if you don't nail the exposure and white balance most of the time, and think you might need to tweak your images later in Photoshop or Photoshop Lightroom. In RAW mode, you can control every aspect of the processing of your images, so if the image is underexposed, overexposed, or has a color problem—you can fix it easily. RAW offers the highest-quality original image, too, and offers maximum flexibility.

TIFF: Shoot in TIFF if you're loose with money. This is a great format for people who have money to burn, people who shoot to huge 16-GB memory cards and have plenty of 'em handy. TIFFs are also perfect for anyone who has lots of spare hard drive space and lots of spare time, because TIFF files are huge to deal with. Outside of that, I can't think of any real compelling (or remotely reasonable) reason to shoot in TIFF format.

Which Size to Shoot In

I recommend shooting at the largest size and highest quality setting that your camera will allow, so if you're shooting in JPEG format, make sure you choose JPEG Fine and a size of Large, so you get the best-quality JPEG image possible. If you choose a lower size, or JPEG Norm (normal), you're literally throwing away quality. The only trade-off is that JPEG Fine photos are a little larger in file size. Not staggeringly larger (those are TIFFs or RAW files)—they're a little larger, but the increase in quality is worth it. If you're serious about getting better-looking photos (and if you bought this book, you are), then set your image size to Large and your JPEG quality to Fine, and you'll be shooting the exact same format many of today's top pros swear by.

WHIMS Will Keep You Out of Trouble

Let's say you're going out shooting landscapes one morning. Do you know what your camera's settings are? They're whatever they were the last time you went shooting. So, if your last shoot was at night, chances are your ISO is set very high, and your white balance is set to whatever you used last. I've gotten burned by this so many times that I had to come up with an acronym to help me remember to check the critical settings on my camera, so I don't mess up an entire shoot (I spent a whole morning in Monument Valley, Utah, shooting at 1600 ISO because I had been shooting a local band the night before). The acronym is WHIMS, which stands for:

W: White balance check
H: Highlight warning turned on
I: ISO check (make sure you're using the right ISO for your surroundings)
M: Mode check (make sure you're in aperture priority, program, or manual mode)
S: Size (check to make sure your image size and quality are set correctly)

Before you take your first shot that day, take 30 seconds and check your WHIMS, and you won't wind up shooting important shots with your camera set to JPEG small (like I did when shooting one day in Taos, New Mexico).

How to Lock Focus

This is another one of those things that has snuck by a lot of people, and that is how to lock your focus. For example, let's say you're lying down, shooting a landscape through some tall grass, and you want the blades of grass in front of you to remain in focus, but when you lift the camera up to get the rest of the scene, the camera refocuses on the background. You can force the camera to keep its focus locked onto those blades of grass by simply holding the shutter button down halfway. While that shutter button is held down, your focus is locked, so now you can recompose the image without your camera trying to refocus on something else. I use this a lot on photos of people who may not be in the center of the frame (it keeps me from having to move the auto-focus dot—I just point at the person, hold the shutter button halfway down to lock the focus, then recompose the shot the way I want it. When it looks good, I just press the shutter button down the rest of the way to take the shot).

Moving Your Point of Focus

SCOTT KELBY

You know how you look through your viewfinder and, in the center of your viewfinder, there's a red circle or a red rectangle? That's your camera's auto-focus (AF) point, and what that point hits winds up being what's in focus. Well, something a lot of people don't realize is that most cameras let you move that focus point up or down, left or right. That way, if you've composed a shot where your subject is standing over to the right side of your frame, you can move the AF point over, right on them, so they wind up being perfectly in focus. On Canon cameras, you move your AF point by using the tiny multi-controller joystick on the back of the camera. On Nikon cameras, you move the AF point by using the multi-selector on the back of the camera.

Zooming in Close? Use a High Shutter Speed

If you're using a long zoom lens, like a 200mm lens, there's something you should know to help you make sure you get sharp photos, and that is—the closer in you zoom, the more any tiny little movement of your lens is exaggerated. So, if you're handholding your camera, and you're shooting zoomed in to 200mm, any little movement on your part and you're going to have some blurry photos. Now, if it's a bright sunny day, you'll probably be shooting at some very fast shutter speeds, which will pretty much neutralize your movement, so you can sidestep that problem. However, if you're shooting in the shade, or really in anything where your shutter speed falls below 1/250 of a second, the best remedy is to put your camera on a tripod (even though it's during the day). That way, you can shoot out at 200mm all day long and not worry about some tiny movement on your part causing a serious loss of sharpness in your shots.

When It's Okay to Erase Your Memory Card

If you only have one memory card, it won't be long before you have to erase that memory card so you can get back to shooting. I have a pretty simple rule I use to know when it's actually okay to erase a memory card, and that is I erase it when I know I have two backup copies of the images that are on it. In other words, I have one set that I copied onto my computer, and then I copied that folder of images over to an external hard drive, so I have two copies. Then, and only then, I feel comfortable erasing that card and shooting again. Remember, when you have just one copy, you're working on the negatives. If your computer's hard drive crashes, those images are gone. Forever. That's why you gotta make a second backup copy, because I've seen people lose their work again and again, year after year, because they didn't make that second backup copy, but don't let that happen to you—back up twice, then erase that card!

Don't Just Delete Your Photos, Reformat the Card

You've probably heard horror stories of people who have done an entire shoot, only to have the memory card go bad and they lose all their shots (if you haven't heard this story—I've got dozens). Anyway, one thing you can do to avoid problems is to not just delete the images on the card (once you've backed up twice), but to format the card in the camera, which erases all the files in the process. Yes, it's that important.

Why You Need to Get in Really Close

SCOTT KELBY

This is probably the single simplest tip in the whole book, and the one that has the potential to make your photography the best, but it's also the one people will resist the most. The tip is: move in close to your subject. Really close. Way closer than you'd think. If you search the Internet, you'll find dozens of references and quotes about how much you can improve your photography by simply getting in closer to your subject. You'll find the famous quote (I'm not sure who it's attributed to) that says (I'm paraphrasing here), "Get your shot set up to where you think you're close enough—then take two steps closer." Or my favorite quote, which I think really sums it up nicely, from famous photographer Robert Capa, who once said, "If your pictures aren't good enough, you're not close enough." The pros know this, practice this, have embraced it, and have passed it on to their students for who knows how long, and yet your average photographer still tries to get "the big picture." Don't be an average photographer, who gets average shots. Take two steps closer, and you'll be two steps closer to better-looking photos.

What to Use Your Histogram For

SCOTT KELBY

Today's dSLRs can display a histogram (which is a graphical reading of the tonal range of your photo) right there on the camera's LCD monitor, but if you don't know how to read one (or didn't know it's there), it doesn't do you much good. I only use my camera's histogram for one thing, and that's to make sure I haven't clipped off any important detail in my highlights. So, what am I looking for when I look at my histogram? Two things: (1) I don't want to see the histogram's graph touch the far right wall. If any of that graph hits the far right wall, I'm losing detail. So, what I'm really hoping to see is (2) a small gap between the end of the histogram and that far right wall (as shown above). If I see that gap, I know I'm okay, and that I'm not clipping any highlights. I can look at my histogram and immediately see if this has happened, and if I have clipped off important highlight information, I will generally use the exposure compensation control on my camera to override what my camera read, and lower the exposure by ⅓ of a stop, then I take the shot again and check my histogram. If I'm still clipping, I lower the exposure compensation to –0.7 and then shoot again, and check again. I keep doing that until my clipping problem goes away. Now, the histogram can only help so much, because what if there's a direct shot of the sun in my photo? That sun will clip big time, and there will be no gap, but that's okay, because the surface of the sun doesn't have any important detail (well, at least as far as I know). So the histogram can help, but it's not the bottom line—you still have to make the call if the area that's clipping is (here's the key phrase) *important detail*, so don't get hung up on histograms—at the end of the day, you have to make the call, and the histogram is just a helper, not your master.

Leave Your Lens Cap Off

My buddy Vinny calls your lens cap "The Never Ready Cap," because whenever that magi-cal once-in-a-lifetime moment happens while you're out shooting, don't worry—it will be long gone by the time you stop and take your lens cap off. I definitely recommend putting your lens cap on when you're storing your gear back in your camera bag, but if your camera is out of that bag, your lens cap needs to be off your camera. If you're wor-ried about scratching your lens, then buy a lens hood (or use the lens hood that came with your lens), but keep that cap off once that camera comes out of your bag.

Removing Spots and Specks After the Fact

If you have a dust spot, smudge, or speck on either your lens or your camera's sensor, you're going to see that spot (or smudge or speck) again and again once you open your photos in Photoshop (or Lightroom, or Elements, etc.). If you want a quick way to get rid of that junk, try Photoshop's (or Elements') Spot Healing Brush tool. All you do is choose it from the Toolbox, then click it once over any spot or speck, and it's gone. That's all there is to it. Now, if you have Photoshop CS3 or higher, and you shot in RAW format, you can fix a bunch of spots all at once (because, after all, if you have a spot on your lens, every shot from your shoot will have that same spot in that exact same location, right?). So, here's what you do: STEP ONE: Select all the photos that are in the same orientation (for example, select all your horizontal shots) and double-click on them to open them in Adobe Camera Raw. STEP TWO: Get Camera Raw's Retouch tool (from the toolbar up top) and click it once right over the spot. This removes that spot from your current photo. STEP THREE: Press the Select All button (on the top left) to select all your other photos, then click the Synchronize button. STEP FOUR: When the dialog appears, from the Synchronize pop-up menu up top, choose Spot Removal, and then click OK. This removes that spot from all your other selected photos automatically. Click Done to save your retouch. STEP FIVE: Open all the photos you took with a tall orientation and do the same thing. Now, all your spots are gone from all your photos in less than two minutes. If you shot 300 or 400 photos—that's sayin' something!

What Looks Good in Black & White

SCOTT KELBY

Some subjects just look great when you convert them from color to black and white, so when you're out shooting, keep an eye out for anything with lots of texture, like the peeling paint on the side of an old building, rusty old machinery, anything with an interesting shape or lots of contrast (because you don't have the crutch of color, you have to look for other things to lead the eye), objects with a lot of metal, old barns, old cars, old abandoned factories, and also consider cloudy days with dark menacing skies a perfect subject for black and white. In fact, any gray nasty day can wind up being a field day for black and white because you don't have to worry about avoiding the sky since it's not a nice, blue, sunny day. In black and white—it's all gray.

Recompose, Don't "Fix It" in Photoshop

SCOTT KELBY

I love Photoshop. I think it totally rocks, and I've written around 35 books on Photo-shop. That being said, it's much faster and easier to get it right in the camera, than it is to fix it later in Photoshop. If you see something distracting in your viewfinder, like a telephone line or a road sign, that's ruining your shot—you certainly could remove either one later in Photoshop. It probably wouldn't take you more than 10 minutes or so to remove that telephone line or road sign in Photoshop. But it probably wouldn't take you more than 10 seconds to move one foot in either direction to recompose your shot so you don't see the telephone wires (or the road sign) at all. Getting it right in the camera is just so much faster, and besides—you want to save your time in Photoshop for finishing your photos, not fixing them. Do yourself a favor, and compose so those distracting elements aren't in your frame, and you'll spend a lot more time shooting and having fun, and a lot less time on tedious cloning and repairing in Photoshop.

Want to Be Taken Seriously? Start Editing

SCOTT KELBY

If you want to be taken seriously as a photographer and you want people to start to view you as a pro-quality photographer, then take a tip from the working pros, which is: only show your very best work. Period. One thing that makes a pro a pro is they're really good photo editors—they're really good at picking, and only showing, their very best stuff. You don't see their so-so shots or the shots that would have been great, if only…. You also don't see them showing seven or eight similar shots of the same subject. Only show your best of the best. That means if you went on a trip and you took 970 shots, you don't come home and show a slide show of 226 images. If you want people to think you're good, show your best 30. If you want people to think you're great, show just your best 10. Think about it: If you took 970 shots, maybe 400 are decent. Out of those decent shots, maybe 80 are pretty good. Out of those 80, maybe 30 are really good. Out of those 30, maybe 10 are outstanding. Now, just show those 10—and blow people away. (Just ask yourself what you would rather see—80 pretty good shots, or 10 outstanding shots.)

How to Be a Great Photo Editor of Your Own Work

Your shots have to stand on their own, without you telling a story about why you like the shot. If you have to explain to someone why you chose it or why you think it's special, it doesn't belong in your portfolio.

Label Your Memory Cards

This is another tip I picked up from Derrick Story, and he tells the true story of how he left a memory card in a taxi cab, but because he always puts a sticker on his cards with his name and address, he was able to get that card returned to him with all the photos still intact. That's right, he lost his memory card in a taxi and got it back. This obviously didn't happen in New York. (I'm totally kidding. You knew that—right?)

Go Square

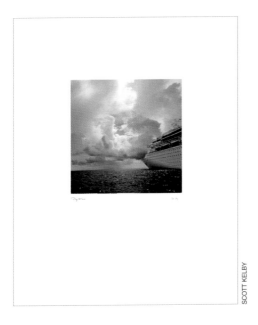

SCOTT KELBY

Today's digital cameras all produce an image that is rectangular, so no matter whose photo you see, it's either a tall rectangle or a wide rectangle. Want to make your photo stand out from the pack and have more of a "fine art" look when you print it? Then "Go square!" That's right—just crop your photo to a perfect square (as seen above), and then position that perfect square with plenty of nice white space around it, for a nice fine art, gallery look, like the layout you see here. It's a simple little thing, but they're all little things, right?

Tip for Shooting at Night (Long Exposure Noise)

If you're shooting at night, your shutter is going to wind up staying open long enough for you to make a good exposure, and depending on how dark it is where you're shooting, it could open for 1/4 of a second, 4 seconds, or 40 seconds. If you start to have long exposures, like 40 seconds, chances are you're going to start to get some serious noise in your photo (even if you were shooting at ISO 100). One thing you can do to help is to turn on your camera's Long Exposure Noise Reduction feature (both Nikon and Canon dSLRs have this feature). This kicks in your camera's built-in noise reduction to combat the kind of noise that shows up in long exposures like these, and they actually do a surprisingly decent job, so they're worth turning on (just in these long exposure instances—this is *not* for everyday use).

Chapter Nine

More Photo Recipes to Help You Get "The Shot"

The Simple Ingredients to Make It All Come Together

The chapter from volume 1 of this book that I probably got the most emails on was this last chapter—the photo recipe chapter. In this chapter, I show some of my shots, and then give the details for how to get a similar shot, including what kind of equipment you'd need, what time to shoot (if it's relevant), where to shoot it, where to set up your lights, tripod, etc., so it's kind of a photo recipe cookbook. Although there are a lot of shooters that do anything to get "the shot," you'll be happy to know—I'm not one of them. In fact, I've often toyed with the idea of starting a trade association for people like me and calling it "The International Society of Convenient Photographers" (or the ISCP, for short). Our credo would be, "Any shot worth getting, is worth driving to." Our ideal situation would be we drive up to a location, roll down the window, take the shot, and drive off. It doesn't get much more convenient than that. There would be special recognition for members who abide by our 50-ft. Cone of Convenience rule, which states: "If a once-in-a-lifetime photographic opportunity presents itself, the member may venture as far as 50 ft. from the member's vehicle, in any one direction, as long as they leave the car's engine running and the air conditioner turned on." But then I realized this was very limiting, because it would exclude most studio photographers. So, we added a special dispensation for them, in rule 153.45, Section B, which states: "A studio photographer should avoid changing their subject's pose, as doing such could force an inconvenient repositioning of the light, which breaks with the sacred tenets of our group." Sure, it's a small group, but we really get around.

The Recipe for Getting This Type of Shot

SCOTT KELBY

Characteristics of this type of shot: A sweeping shot with a silky waterfall effect, with lots of detail front-to-back and a real sense of depth. (*Note:* The location is Yosemite Falls.)

(1) To get this type of sweeping look, you need to use a very-wide-angle lens. This was shot with a 12mm wide-angle (it's not a fisheye lens—just a super-wide-angle).

(2) To get the detail from front to back, shoot in aperture priority (Av) mode and choose the highest number f-stop you can (this was shot at f/22, which keeps everything in focus from front to back).

(3) You absolutely need to shoot on a tripod for a shot like this because you're shooting at f/22, which means your shutter will be open long enough that even a tiny bit of movement will make the photo blurry.

(4) Another benefit of shooting at f/22 is that since your shutter stays open longer, the water in the waterfall looks silky (you might remember this trick from volume 1 of this book—how to get that smooth, silky water effect). You'll also want to use a cable release (or your camera's self-timer function), so you don't add any blur when pressing the shutter button (yes, it makes a difference).

(5) The final key to this shot is shooting it right around dawn. This does two things, the first being that since it's darker outside, your shutter will stay open longer and your water will look silkier. You couldn't get that silky water look at 1:00 in the afternoon. The second thing is even more important: the quality of the light and the nice soft shadows only happen like this around dawn (and around sunset), so get up early and get the shot!

The Recipe for Getting This Type of Shot

SCOTT KELBY

Characteristics of this type of shot: Very shallow depth of field (the front of the plate is out of focus, so is the back). The subject looks very sharp and the lighting is just great.

(1) Ask to sit near a window with natural light. This shot was taken in a restaurant, and before we were seated I asked the host to seat us near a window. There was a booth against a window, facing north, and as we passed it, I asked if we could have that booth. They were happy to oblige. Then, position the food so the light is hitting the food from the side (this helps to add depth and dimension to your shot).

(2) To capture food this close, you'll need a macro or close-up lens. I used a Canon Close-Up Lens screwed onto a Nikon 17–55mm f/2.8 lens (see Chapter 7 of this book or Chapter 2 of volume 1 for more on close-up lenses), but you can also use a regular macro lens or the macro setting on a zoom lens (if yours has one).

(3) Macro and close-up lenses already have a very shallow depth of field, but to get this look (with the plate out of focus in front and in back), shoot at the lowest number f-stop you can (like f/2.8 or f/4).

(4) When you're using a macro filter, you really need to use a tripod to keep your subject sharp like this, and in this case I used a very small Bogen tabletop tripod, barely big enough to hold my camera.

(5) To minimize any blur, use your camera's self-timer feature to take the shot for you (it might look especially weird to be using a cable release in a restaurant).

The Recipe for Getting This Type of Shot

SCOTT KELBY

Characteristics of this type of shot: Soft, beautiful, natural light, very directional, and the shadows on the darker side of the face aren't too dark.

(1) The key to this shot is the light, and to get this gorgeous light, just position your subjects about 6 feet from a north-facing window. You also want to position them a little bit back behind the window, so they don't get the direct light, but only the edge of the light (that's where it's the softest and most flattering).

(2) To keep from having really dark shadows on the side of their faces that are facing away from the window, put a silver reflector just to the right of your subjects (from the camera view)—as close to them as possible without actually seeing it in the photo. You can position it straight up and down (like a wall beside them), and just a little in front of them (so the reflected light falls mostly on the front of them, not the back).

(3) This is a little bit of a low-light situation, so you're better off shooting this on a tripod for the maximum sharpness in the photo.

(4) To get this level of closeness from your subjects, use the trick I talked about in Chapter 3 for getting your subjects to pose closer than they normally would.

(5) Stand back at least 10 to 12 feet from your subjects and use a zoom lens to shoot somewhere around the 110mm to 140mm range, which looks great for portraits.

The Recipe for Getting This Type of Shot

SCOTT KELBY

Characteristics of this type of shot: Soft, natural-looking lighting, a bright background, sharp details in the features, and the whole photo seems to have energy.

(1) This was taken on a white seamless background (the model is my news anchor on *Photoshop User TV,* Stephanie Cross), and to make the background look nice and white, you need to aim a flash (or studio strobe) directly at the background. Place it behind your subject so their body covers the flash and stand. If you're using a flash meter, you'd like this background to read at least one stop brighter than your subject reads (so if you hold a light meter under her chin, aim it back at the camera, do a meter reading, and it shows f/11, when you walk back and take a reading from the background, it should read f/16. If it doesn't, turn up the power of the background flash and take another reading, and repeat this process until it reads f/16).

(2) This was shot with only one light and reflector (but it was one heck of a light). I used a 7' Elinchrom Octabank softbox, and it's positioned to her right, in front of her at a 45° angle. To get the extremely soft light you see here, you have to use a very large softbox and (this is key) position it as close to her as you possibly can.

(3) To keep the shadows from being too dark on the side of her face that is facing away from the light, use a silver reflector to bounce some of the light from that huge softbox back towards her.

(4) To get that movement in her hair, just turn on a fan and aim it at her. Easy enough.

The Recipe for Getting This Type of Shot

Characteristics of this type of shot: Dramatic portrait, suited for male subjects, with lots of drama to the lighting. Tight cropping gives the image impact.

(1) To get this type of shot, you need a dedicated flash, like a Nikon SB-800 (which this shot was taken with), or a Canon 580EX or EX II.

(2) To get the directional light, you have to get the flash off the camera, and to get it off the camera this far, you have to use either wireless flash or a really long sync cable.

(3) To get the softness and wrapping quality of the light from the flash, you'll need to fire the flash through a diffuser (this shot was taken with a flash fired through a Lasto-lite TriGrip 1 Stop Diffuser mounted on a light stand).

(4) Position the light to the right of the camera, at about a 45° angle toward your subject. Then put the diffusion panel as close as you can get it to your subject without actually seeing it in the photo. Put your flash about 1 foot behind the panel.

(5) No reflector is necessary and no tripod is necessary (the flash will freeze your subject).

The Recipe for Getting This Type of Shot

SCOTT KELBY

Characteristics of this type of shot: Glassy, still water, a beautiful sky, rich colors, and a wide vista.

(1) The key to this shot is (once again) when you shoot it. This type of shot needs to be taken about 30 minutes after sunset (everybody else will have already packed up by then, but sometimes the best light happens well after sunset). Also, composing so the horizon line is in the lower third of the frame really adds to its sweeping feel.

(2) In low light like this, of course, you need to shoot on a tripod and use a cable release or your camera's self-timer to minimize any camera shake. Because you're on a tripod, you can shoot at ISO 100, which will minimize any noise.

(3) You'll need to use a wide-angle lens to capture this wide a view (this was taken with a 12–24mm f/2.8 lens set at 19mm).

(4) This is another one of those shots where you want to use f/8 or a higher number to keep as much in focus as possible.

(5) There's only one way to get that smooth, glassy water, and that's to be lucky. This was taken at Cape Porpoise, Maine, and for three straight days there was just no wind, and the water in the cove you see above was just like glass. Sometimes you have to be patient and go back to a location a number of times, if you can, to finally shoot it when the sky looks great and the water is glassy. Once those two things come together, then follow steps 1–4 and you'll get a shot just like this.

The Recipe for Getting This Type of Shot

SCOTT KELBY

Characteristics of this type of shot: A daylight shot with the sun being overpowered with flash, and while the flash is bright, it's not harsh.

(1) This was taken at around 3:30 or 4:00 in the afternoon, in the middle of a major league ballpark (right after the game), and when the light is harsh like this, you can either put a diffuser (a translucent piece of fabric) between the sun and your subject (which puts them in the shade) or use a flash to overpower the sun, which is what I did here. The flash is actually positioned to his right (from the camera view) just outside the frame of the photo (in fact, it's on a light stand in front of seat 5 in the front row). (2) To keep the light from the flash from being harsh, place that diffuser between the flash and your subject. So, he's seated in seat 11. In his same row, in seat 13, is a Lasto-lite TriGrip diffuser connected to a light stand. It's literally just out of reach of his hand on the right side (from the camera view). Then, the flash (on a light stand) is one row in front of that, firing at him through that diffuser to make the light from the flash softer. (3) To capture your subject, and the surroundings, use a wide-angle lens (this was taken with a 17–55mm f/2.8 lens set at 44mm, so it's not too wide). To keep the fore-ground and background in focus, use f/8 or a higher number. (4) Since this was shot using flash, which freezes any motion, no tripod is necessary. (5) Since this was taken in daylight, using ISO 100 (for the least noise and maximum sharpness) was no problem.

The Recipe for Getting This Type of Shot

SCOTT KELBY

Characteristics of this type of shot: Beautiful, wrapping light, with a nice dramatic shadow on the far side of the face.

(1) This shot couldn't be easier, because it's mostly natural light coming in through a window. Usually, we'd place our subject farther away from the window to get softer light, but because the light was already heavily softened by the stained glass, we were able to position her closer to the window.

(2) If you want the stained glass to be an important part of the photo (which we did here), position yourself away from the window and shoot back towards the window.

(3) The only other thing you need to make this work is a silver reflector to the left of the subject (from the camera view), just far enough away that it's not in the photo. That helped to keep the shadow side of her face from being too dark.

The Recipe for Getting This Type of Shot

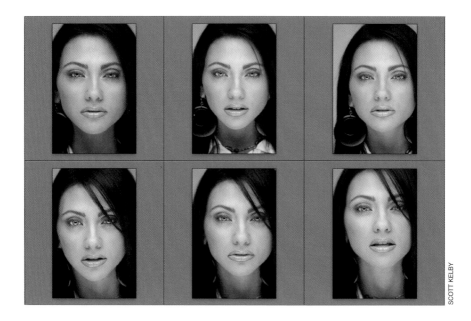

SCOTT KELBY

Characteristics of this type of shot: A bright, clean flash/beauty look with minimal shadows (mostly a small shadow under the nose), with bright, well-lit eyes that sparkle.

(1) Believe it or not, this is a one-light setup that is incredibly easy to use and gets wonderful results. You position the softbox directly in front of your subject, just a little higher than your subject's head, and tilted back down toward your subject (so the light is coming from slightly above her head). The key is to place this softbox absolutely as close as you can get it to your subject without being seen in the photo (so it may be only 8 or 10 inches from their face).

(2) Now, you take a silver reflector, hold it flat in front of your subject (like a dish), right at their chest level, so it reflects the light from the softbox just above their forehead and fills their face with this beautiful light. Put this as close as you can to your subject without it showing up in the frame.

(3) This setup is often referred to as clamshell lighting, because it looks like a giant clam that's about to eat your subject's face (strange as that may sound).

(4) There will be a little gap between the softbox and your reflector, and you position your camera to shoot between that gap, which gives you the look you see above, which has very little shadow, thanks to the light bouncing back into your subject's face.

The Recipe for Getting This Type of Shot

SCOTT KELBY

Characteristics of this type of shot: Dramatic light, lots of detail and depth.

(1) This shot is all about the light, because after all—it's just a shot of a boot. But it's a boot in really, really good light. This is natural light from a window with a very, very sheer drape in front of it, which helped soften the light.

(2) The key to making the light go where you want it is to block out the parts of the light you don't want. The top of his leg is darker because we blocked some of the light with the table the cowboy was sitting at, so it mostly fell right where we wanted it to— on the boot. You can block window light with pretty much anything you have handy (a jacket, a sweater, your camera bag, etc.).

(3) Although there are parts of this photo that are bright (like the floor behind his boot, and the highlights on his boot), this is definitely a low-light shot, and should be taken on a tripod for sure.

(4) The reason the photo has a yellowish look to it is because the white balance was set to something very warm (the Cloudy setting), which does a nice job of making everything just that little bit warmer, and is especially useful for outdoor shots (I leave my white balance set to Cloudy for all my outdoor shots. But then again, I shoot in RAW, so if I don't like the way Cloudy looks, I can always change the white balance later in Adobe Camera Raw).

The Recipe for Getting This Type of Shot

SCOTT KELBY

Characteristics of this type of shot: Dramatic beams of light, a photo with lots of depth and mystery.

(1) The trick to photographing beams of light is to take two handfuls of sand, toss them up into the air near the beams, and after a few seconds the beams will start to clearly appear as the sand starts to settle (this happens just after the sand hits the floor). I had a friend doing the sand tossing—he tossed it up, then quickly moved out of the frame. (2) For you to see beams of light, you're going to have to be in a place that's dark enough for beams to appear (in this case, I'm down in a small underground room [called a kiva] in New Mexico's Pecos National Historical Park). In low light like this, you'll have to be on a tripod to keep from having very blurry photos, because your shutter will have to stay open long enough to get a decent exposure (my shutter speed in this shot was 1/10 of a second). (3) To get the ladder in the foreground (which you use to climb down into the kiva) in focus, and have the back wall of the kiva in focus, you need to use an f-stop like f/8 or a higher number (the higher the number, the more of the photo will be in focus). (4) The last thing is this: with all that sand floating around, you can protect your camera from getting too dirty by wrapping it in a plastic shower cap (like the kind you'll find in your hotel room), so just the lens is sticking out. It works wonders to keep most of the dirt out.

The Recipe for Getting This Type of Shot

SCOTT KELBY

Characteristics of this type of shot: Great color and reflection in the window. A clear subject, and depth created by the grass being in front of the window.

(1) There are two keys to this shot, the first being composition. This was a window on the side of an old garage/barn, and you could try to capture the entire barn, but that's really tough. Instead, by closing in tight and focusing in on just one element of the large barn, it creates a very clear subject and a simple image with impact.

(2) The other key to this shot is positioning the camera so you see as much reflected sky as possible (I moved up and down the side of the building until I could find a spot where the reflection pretty much filled the window).

(3) This shot was taken very late in the day on the shady side of the barn, so that means lower light, which means you need to shoot it on a tripod (to keep from having a blurry photo). Also, to get the blades of grass in the shot, you have to position your camera at a very low angle, so you're basically down in the grass (I had to shoot this on my knees, with my camera aiming up a bit at the window, and the window was actually pretty low on the side of the barn). It was shot with a 17–55mm zoom lens, set at 40mm at f/11. Because of the low light, the shutter speed was 1/40 of a second (if the camera had read 1/60 of a second, I could have possibly gotten away with shooting handheld, but it still wouldn't be as sharp as taking it on a tripod, where there's no movement at all).

The Recipe for Getting This Type of Shot

SCOTT KELBY

Characteristics of this type of shot: This is one of the product shots for the book, which I lit to have lots of depth and detail, and the reflection below it is actually real.

(1) This was shot on a table on white seamless background paper. The way to get the reflection is to put a large sheet of clear plexiglass over the paper, and then anything you put on it creates a nice reflection. It's simple, but it works.

(2) To light a product like this so it doesn't look flat and boring, you'll need more than one light (in this case, three lights). One strobe with a softbox is placed to the camera's left, aiming back at the product about 2 feet in front of it. A second light is placed diagonally behind the product to the camera's right. The third light is actually a long strip bank we normally use as a hair light (like the one shown in Chapter 2), but a regular small softbox would have been perfect. So, why we did we use a strip bank? Honestly, it was because it was handy—it was already set up on a boom stand from a portrait shoot the day before, so we did the "lazy photographer" thing and used what was convenient. We placed the light directly above the product. Also, I used Westcott TD5 Spiderlites, which are those continuous daylight balanced fluorescent lights that are ideal for product photography (shot at ISO 200 at f/8 at 1/20 of a second).

(3) The goal when lighting a shot like this is to have areas that have lots of highlights and other areas with shadows. If it doesn't, the product looks flat.

(4) This was shot from far back with a 70–200mm lens all the way out at 200mm.

The Recipe for Getting This Type of Shot

Characteristics of this type of shot: Close-up shot with a dramatic black background, and lots of detail and depth for a close-up shot like this.

(1) If you want a solid black background behind a flower, you have to put one there (I used a Westcott Collapsible Illuminator background, like the one in Chapter 2). The background is about 4 feet behind the flower.

(2) If you want beautiful flowers to shoot, buy 'em (I went to a local florist and ordered pink and yellow Gerbera daisies, which came in within two days. If the florist knows you're buying them to photograph them, they usually make sure you get really beautiful selections).

(3) This is taken with a macro lens, and to get this much depth of field you have to follow all three macro rules, including shooting at the highest aperture possible (f/22, in this case), shooting on a tripod, and shooting with the barrel of the lens aiming straight at the subject (not tipping up or down—perfectly horizontal).

(4) The light is nothing but beautiful, late afternoon, summer light. No reflectors, no flash—just natural light under the awning of a house (so it's not direct light).

(5) What makes this shot interesting is that you're showing a view of a daisy that's rarely seen—the underside of the back of the flower. To get this view, I had to place the vase on a tall side table, so I could get the camera low enough to be below the back of the flower.

The Recipe for Getting This Type of Shot

SCOTT KELBY

Characteristics of this type of shot: Golden, beautiful light, nice reflections in the windows, and a wide sweeping look.

(1) The key to getting this look is when you shoot it, you have to be in place and ready to shoot at dawn.

(2) For a sweeping look like this, you need to use a wide-angle zoom lens (this was shot with a 17–55mm zoom lens, set at 22mm). To keep a decent amount of focus throughout the shot, you should choose f/8 or a higher number (f/11, f/16, etc.).

(3) Since you're shooting just after dawn, the light will be low and your shutter will stay open longer (the shutter stayed open for 1/8 of a second), so you absolutely need to shoot this type of shot on a tripod or your shot will be blurry. Also, use a cable release or your camera's self-timer to minimize any camera shake.

(4) To get the reflections in the windows, you literally just have to walk around and position yourself at an angle where the reflections show up in the windows as much as possible.

(5) Since you're shooting on a tripod, shoot at 100 ISO for maximum quality and clarity.

(6) Because your subject has lots of white in it (the exterior walls), make sure your camera's highlight (clipping) warning is turned on, and if you get areas that are blinking when you view them in your LCD monitor, use your camera's exposure compensation control to lower the exposure by 1/3 of a stop or more, then shoot again.

The Recipe for Getting This Type of Shot

SCOTT KELBY

Characteristics of this type of shot: Dramatic portrait shot, ideal for shots of men due to the dark shadows on the right side of the face.

(1) The key to this shot is where you position the softbox. The camera is aiming straight forward, right at the subject, but you have the subject look to your left. The softbox isn't right in front of where he's looking—it's actually positioned a little bit past him, so the side of his face that is turned away from the camera is getting the direct light.
(2) Since you're on the other side of the light, it puts the camera side of his face in shadow, like you see here.
(3) Don't use a reflector to open up the shadows on the side of his face nearest the camera—you want that to be dark and fully in shadow, like you see here. That's it—one softbox—it's all in where you place it.

Index

A

air travel, 160
aperture priority mode, 52, 99, 180
auto-focus
  moving AF point, 186
  turning off, 169

B

backgrounds
  black, 62
  collapsible, 57
  color saturated, 62
  lighting, 59, 60, 63
  macro photography, 173
  out-of-focus, 99
  portrait, 80, 99
  studio, 36, 57, 59
  white, 59, 63
backlight
  flower photos and, 123
  outdoor portraits and, 75
  wedding photos and, 131
battery grips, 74
battery pack, 144
Black, Dave, 24
black backgrounds, 62
black flags, 68
black reflectors, 64, 68
black-and-white images
  shots conducive to, 193
  wedding photos converted to, 140
bounce card, 18
bouncing light, 15, 96
bridal portraits
  backlighting, 131
  bridal gown in, 143
  posing the bride, 142
  profile shots, 146
  See also **wedding photos**

C

Camera Raw, 135
cameras. *See* **digital cameras**
Canon wireless flash, 11–12, 28
Capa, Robert, 189
casual group shots, 85
chairs for portraits, 93

cityscapes, 157
close-up lens attachment, 175
collapsible background, 57
colors
  background, 62
  reflector, 64, 98
composing photos, 194
  portraits, 81, 82
  wedding pictures, 139
continuous light, 44
couple portraits, 97
Cross, Stephanie, 205

D

Dantzig, Stephen, 67
dappled light, 95
dedicated flash, 6
depth of field, 99, 168
diffusion dome, 14
diffusion panel, 16–17, 79
digital cameras
  full-frame, 124
  orientation of, 73, 77
Digital ProTalk **blog,** 148
directional light, 7
drag-the-shutter technique, 13

E

editing your photos, 195
egg crate grid, 51
exposure compensation, 115
extension tubes, 177
eyes
  minimizing shadows under, 100
  twinkle added to, 18

F

facial fixes, 90
famous landmarks, 158–159
fans, studio, 54
fast lenses, 137, 163
feathering light, 55
filters, polarizer, 105, 118
fisheye lenses, 112
flash, 1–32
  battery pack, 144
  bounce card, 18
  dedicated, 6
  distance for using, 29–30
  drag-the-shutter technique, 13
  dramatic light from, 31

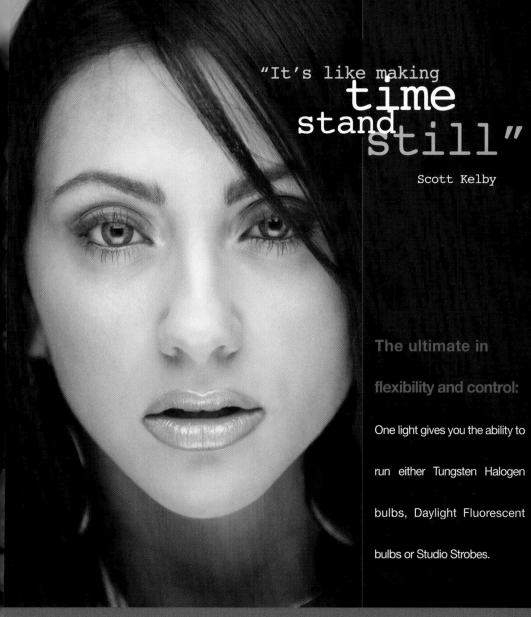

"It's like making **time** stand *still*"

Scott Kelby

The ultimate in

flexibility and control:

One light gives you the ability to

run either Tungsten Halogen

bulbs, Daylight Fluorescent

bulbs or Studio Strobes.

Photography by Scott Kelby using the Spiderlite® TD5 by **westcott**®

Images courtesy of iStockphoto

It's not magic...
it's Photoshop!

Sometimes the perfect photo just happens...everything captured in its
exact detail. And, other times there's Photoshop...
Every day the National Association of Photoshop Professionals shows
thousands of photographers around the world how to turn ordinary
into extraordinary...moments into memories...pictures into art.

Join today and receive...

8 issues of *Photoshop User* magazine • unlimited access
to the members-only website and its massive collection of online tutorials
• exclusive member-only discounts • online tech support, and much more.
Plus, as a bonus, you'll get "The Best of *Photoshop User*: The Ninth Year" DVD
One-Year Membership $99* • **Two-Year Membership $179***
Use code NAPM-1UM for your gift.

National Association of Photoshop Professionals
The ultimate resource for Adobe® Photoshop® training, education, news, and more.